"From my perspective through the lens of the banking industry, this book is revolutionary!"

-Michael Metcalf, Bank Operations Analyst, BMO Harris

"Mike Wolf is presenting information here that not only is in keeping with IRS Rules for compliance, but it makes my job a whole lot eaasier."

-Robert Nettles, IRS Enrolled Agent

"Kanketa finance merges traditional accounting with everyday practicality. An ingenious, long-awaited solution is to age-old money management probles that continue to plague small business owners everywhere."

-Clark Crosby CEO Cell-Sync Neutraceutical Corporation

"The practices here are keeping our company safe and growing while the industry struggles with huge price fluctuations. I remember this book to every small busniess owner."

- Ed Puzia, President, AAA Pipe and Fittings

"Yeah! No more guesswork! This is our new business bible. I'd give this two thumbs up but I need one to turn the pages!"

- Stephanie, CEO, Ascend Elevator

"A unique, easy to use, result driven methodology (KENKETA) which is the science of operating a small business. I would highly recommend the use of KANKETA for any small business."

- Nick Carrocia, Director IBM International Training

BUSINESS RECOVERY in DIFFICULT TIMES

MIKE WOLF

authorHOUSE®

AuthorHouse™
1663 Liberty Drive
Bloomington, IN 47403
www.authorhouse.com
Phone: 833-262-8899

Published by AuthorHouse 12/19/2020

ISBN: 978-1-6655-0733-2 (sc)
ISBN: 978-1-6655-0734-9 (hc)
ISBN: 978-1-6655-0754-7 (e)

Library of Congress Control Number: 2020922339

Print information available on the last page.

Any people depicted in stock imagery provided by Getty Images are models,
and such images are being used for illustrative purposes only.
Certain stock imagery © Getty Images.

This book is printed on acid-free paper.

Because of the dynamic nature of the Internet, any web addresses or links contained in
this book may have changed since publication and may no longer be valid. The views
expressed in this work are solely those of the author and do not necessarily reflect the
views of the publisher, and the publisher hereby disclaims any responsibility for them.

NO TIME FOR HARVARD? NO SWEAT!

KANKETA™

This isn't just another approach to traditional financial management. Kanketa is an eastern based business management philosophy that has been proven over decades, in the best of times and the worst of times.

The Kanketa Balanced Budget is a uniquely formed, highly crafted, method for managing money. It will give you all day-to-day financial strategies that you will need for the rest of your professional career, regardless of where your business takes you.

ALL THE FINANCE YOU'LL EVER NEED
TO RUN A SAFE, PROFITABLE SMALL BUSINESS

<u>GUARANTEED!</u>

My sincerest gratitude

to the 72 executives
of global companies
for your time, energy, effort,
tireless passion and commitment
to helping me form and prove
these concepts

And ...   to all Business Leaders
who are hungry for knowledge,
humble enough to explore change,
smart enough to recognize
and take advantage of
the proven practices of others,
and courageous enough to implement them

I am eternally grateful.

CONTENTS

MONEY KEPT

MONEY MANAGED

Every business problem that exists, or has ever existed
is the result of one area of a company
out of balance with another.

All solutions can be found by
putting the company into balance with itself.

Balance internally, and the external forces will follow.
Balance the company, and you will solve the problem.

Mike Wolf

 # FORETHOUGHT

Writing this book was the single most difficult thing I have ever done in this amount of time. These pages demanded arduous effort from every fiber of my being. Over the last six months since COVID hit, my sentiments have changed weekly. I began with a view of an out-of-balance world that seemed to be rebalancing. I saw greedy hoarders sharing and helping. I observed creativity abounding in every crack and crevice of our society. Through my lens, people everywhere began looking at each other instead of looking away. I noticed that folks of all ages and walks of life were generally slowing down and re-assessing what is really important. I had just completed my final thoughts, when protesters hit the streets. Businesses everywhere were looted and damaged. The Constitution of our country is being challenged daily. Our legal system is being rocked at its foundation. Laws are morphing weekly. Our leaders continue to wobble. Hope of restoration of order is unraveling. From week to week I can't identify who would ever take time to read or even be interested in the material in this book.

I decided to rescue myself and return to the basics. I began with the premise that our country was founded on small businesses. There are universal principles that have built and guided mom and pop shops into mega giant success stories through the worst of times. One thing is certain. There will always be business, and a need for your services. And as long as there is business, there will always room for this material.

It's no secret that global, national, regional, local, neighborhood disasters take down businesses. This book hit the press in the middle of COVID19, in an ever-evolving world. It could have been published during Y2K, 911, SARS, HIVAIDS, Ebola, the housing crash, amid a tsunami in New Orleans, or a touchdown of a tornado in Kansas. It could have been released at any moment of social and economic abnormality.

In the context of everyday business, there is also a global re-engineering. The New Normal (if there is such a thing) is demanding a redesign of our worn and dated business habits in ways that we do not yet understand. I come with years of personal proof that the information here is more critical than ever for business safety and survival.

Anyone who is now faced with recovering and rebuilding their business has a second chance, a fresh start to course correct, and do it right with new tools.

In another sense, this isn't necessarily about business recovering from a pandemic. Neither is this exclusively written for the rescue of a small business in need of help in the recovery process. More appropriately, this is the first of a three-book trilogy about setting a small business on a straight and narrow path and managing it safely and properly.

BOOK 1: BUSINESS RECOVERY in DIFFICULT TIMES.
This book will help you to redesign your business beginning with finance. Book 1 will show you how to construct a perfect and lasting budget for your business. You will closely examine each of six primary money components that create a balanced budget to keep your business safe from sudden and unforeseen market changes that unexpectedly interrupt your progress and your profitability.

BOOK 2: THE FUTURE OF SMALL BUSINESS MANAGEMENT, POST COVID19
Why is it that eastern companies rarely have layoffs in the worst of economic turmoil? Book 2 gives you a crystal ball for your business that allows you to see into the future. This book introduces you to the Kanketa Scorecard; a tool that gives you the ability to see your financial limitations clearly so that you can make good, everyday business decisions and reliably predict and act on problems *before* they happen.

BOOK 3: THE MOST CRITICAL NUMBER IN YOUR BUSINESS (It's is not profit).
Profit is the result of this more important number. Book 3 presents a quick formula that accurately measures the success and value of any business at any given moment in time and gives proven ways to course correct problems. Book 3 is highly valuable to anyone who is considering exiting or retiring within the next five years. Book three takes you on a journey toward the end game to increase your business value in order to sell or lease your business to the highest bidder.

BUSINESS RECOVERY IN DIFFICULT TIMES

THIS BOOK is dedicated to maintaining financial safety and managing a small business before a calamity. Every business has always been and will always be in need of what you will find between these covers. Business safety is unconditionally timeless.

These pages are about money. Your hard-earned money. The money that feeds your family. The money that runs your small business every day. It is also a book for passionate, skillful people who are uncomfortable with or confused by money talk. I want you to know upfront that this information will require a desire to grow your business and the willingness to make changes. One thing is irrefutable. Real success begins at the end of your comfort zone.

My goal is to change how you think about your business. I do not want you to have the sleepless nights worrying about payroll like I did in my companies. I want all the mystery and guesswork that might be creating errors and costing you time and money to disappear. I want you to be able to add more time and enjoyment to your day. The more you can streamline your finances, the more freedom you will have to do what you do best with less stress. I want you to always have enough money to keep your business healthy and growing. Put these principles in motion and you will work less and earn more, while your financial system runs itself.

Just think of how great it would be if

SOMEDAY,

all owners of small businesses will
manage their companies passionately,
in an error-free environment
without the stress, mystery and guesswork
associated with business finance.

This is my vision.

This information is different. Very different.

I guarantee that you will not find the information in this book anywhere else. It is not taught in the most expensive business schools. It is not learned on the job. It is not passed down from parents. It was painfully gleaned from over a half century of working with global corporations. No single company provided all the material. It took over 300 companies contributing their fair share. Seventy-two executives from Fortune 1000 companies stepped up to the plate to help me to prove the results. So, I guess, you can say that, in one sense, what you are reading here is still a big secret in the circles of businesspeople you know.

You're going to look and sound very, very smart when you talk about this. And even better... your business will become very safe in the process. The results of this book could come quickly. The ideas are easy to understand and can be immediately used with surprising results. I don't want you to worry or wonder whether you are doing things right. So, I put my phone number in the final pages of this book for you to call, with any questions at no cost. Additionally, I will make certain tools available to you, again at no cost. This information can change the world and you can help to spread the word.

The real secret to the success of your business is financial balance. Financial balance means putting the right amount of money in the right places at the right times for the right purposes, and for all the right reasons. Your success is embedded in how you think about money and how well you put these principles to work.

Why A Balanced Budget?

A balanced budget is like the training wheels on a bike. It keeps your business from falling down when unexpected market changes constantly surprise you; social change, technological change, economic change, changes in the environment, and all the political, legal, ethical, demographic changes in age, education and income that blind side you. At any given moment, your business is being undermined by unforeseen, uncontrollable factors. A balanced budget is your suit of armor to weather the storms that constantly threaten your business and put it at risk.

Financial Balance

Financial Balance is fundamental. The six components of financial balance will help you to create a useful and meaningful Profit and Loss Statement that is different than the one you might be using today. A balanced budget will expose limitations and prevent overspending.

Get the Most Out of This Book.

At first glance, there appears to be a lot of detail in these pages. Fair enough. There is. And there is nothing in here that should go unsaid. But, please, whatever you do, don't sweat the details! They will come over time. Keep to the big picture.

The best overview is the Table of Contents. Also, look for the call-out boxes along the way for applied practices. Additionally, the final chapter presents a summary of all concepts for easy reference. Above all, be courageous.

This is a fresh, carefully crafted and uniquely formed approach to financial management and a prescription for success.

If you choose to pursue Kanketa philosophies and decide to put these practices to work in your business, I promise that you will exponentially reap their rewards as I did. This system will save you decades of guesswork, and maybe save your business.

The good news is that you don't have to do everything all at once to enjoy immediate benefits. Do what is comfortable first. Dip your toe in or go for a splash. Feel confident knowing that whatever you do is bringing you closer to becoming a safe, high-performing company.

24 Questions. 24 Answers.

To the best of my experience and ability, I will deliver specific answers to fundamental questions that have helped me to survive and thrive in every economic swing. These questions continue to plague the minds of many small business owners who have not yet read this book. To put this to work for you is your choice, your decision and your outcomes.

QUESTIONS THAT THIS BOOK ANSWERS:

CHAPTER 1

NUMBERS DON'T LIE

Men lie. Women lie. Kids lie. Numbers don't. From all that you have read about financial statements and heard from advisors and planners and from all the information on the web from self-appointed "experts", how would you ever know who or what to believe? Here's some <u>real</u> good advice. Don't believe anyone. Not accountants. Not financial advisors. Not banks. Not me. Trust yourself first. Trust your logic and trust your instincts. If it makes good sense to you, do it. If it doesn't, put it aside.

It's not the numbers that are lying to you. Be careful that you don't lie to the numbers that you see.
If the numbers say the month won't turn out ok, believe it.
If the numbers say you aren't growing, believe it.
If the numbers say you aren't having a good year, believe it.
What small business owners tend to do is ignore the numbers in front of them and go into denial because they want their businesses to work. Instead they will say...

"I THINK this month will turn out ok."
"It SEEMS like we are growing."
"It FEELS like we'll have a good year."
"I THINK we're profitable."
"I HOPE we can afford it."
"We'll PROBABLY end up ahead of last year."

Think? Feel? Hope? Pray? Maybe? Probably? These aren't the words of a confident business owner who sees numbers that show the truth. Believe your numbers and act on them in enough time to fix the problem before the problem can no longer be fixed.

Every concept presented here will be reduced to a number. Every idea will produce specific, quantifiable, reliably predictable outcomes. Measurable results are what the Kanketa system creates. Nothing more. Nothing less. What you do with the results is up to you.

THE 30-DAY BUSINESS

Kanketa is designed to manage a business one month at a time. The previous month is history. The coming month hasn't happened yet.

Think of it like this. Your business restarts at midnight on the first day of every month and ends at 11:59 pm. on the last day of the month. During that time, you have either made or lost money. Wash. Rinse. Repeat.

A year is twelve one-month periods strung together with twelve opportunities to win or lose. Last month's outcome is a worthless, uncontrollable slice of history. Everything outside of the immediate 30-day performance cycle is irrelevant.

There is nothing else.

THE PROBLEM WITH GAAP ACCOUNTING

**"Death and Taxes have merged.
My financial statements show a profit.
Why isn't it in my checking account?"**

We, in the U.S.A., are subject to something called GAAP accounting (Generally Accepted Accounting Principles). Unfortunately, GAAP leaves a big GAP in how business owners think about money. GAAP was invented for the convenience of the IRS. In my opinion, GAAP is not useful for small business decision-making.

All accountants are exclusively trained in the GAAP system. That is how they got their government license to practice. GAAP has its own accounting language and is exclusively taught in all U.S. business schools.

Like 95% of the rest of the small business owners in the US., you probably didn't go to accounting school. So, this is how your accountant will sound to you when they talk about your finances:

"framistans kj skjfhskj debt to income jhkj snerbs and retained earnings for the last fiscal year finorng and that's not a good return on investment snibit, snibit .... so, pay these taxes next week, or else!"

The financial statements provided to you by your accountant are created for IRS tax-compliance purposes. Certainly, efficiency is necessary for the stability of our country and its economy. GAAP provides an easy, organized reporting format to the government. But GAAP financial statements are not good business planning tools.

The eastern-based Kanketa money management method has a better way to learn about, talk about, and use money in your business.

GAAP Problem #1: The Alphabet

The list of income and expenses that the government and the financial industry uses is your Profit & Loss statement, commonly referred to as the "P&L".

The business expenses under GAAP are usually arranged alphabetically according to expense types: **A**dvertising, **B**ank fees, **C**leaning service, **D**elivery, etc. Alphabetical order might help to process taxes efficiently, but it masks the importance of items when balancing a budget.

There is nothing wrong with alphabetical indexing for quick identification of an expense. But if the expenses on your P&L were organized differently to give you better definition and clarity about how your business is performing, and if your business would be safer, and more profitable as a result, wouldn't you want to use that system, instead?

Kanketa uses the same numbers as GAAP, but with different labels to create a better outcome.

GAAP Problem #2: All Businesses Are Created Equal

GAAP accounting rules use the exact same accounting procedures for Larry's Landscaping and Garden Supply, a small family-owned business, as they do for IBM, General Motors, Coca Cola and the rest. It must be remembered that Certified Public Accountants are contracted by, and work for the Federal Government. It says so right in their license to practice. They are sworn to uphold government tax laws and protect government interests.

No one wants to be non-compliant and get in trouble with the IRS. Many small business owners completely turn their books over to some accountant to take care of everything, believing they are avoiding trouble. No questions asked.

It is important to know that accountants do not hold pixie dust and are not a golden guarantee that you will avoid IRS trouble. An accountant is your first-pass, proofreader of your tax situation before you enter the lion's den. They will spot little things here and there. But accountants can often just as easily create bigger problems because they do not and never will understand your business as well as you do.

You pay an accountant to fill out government forms accurately. That is their service. Maybe you are buying this service because you might be afraid to make a mistake. Maybe you don't have the time, interest or inclination to do them yourself. Remember that the forms are not designed for accountants. They are designed by the government to be independently used by the everyday U.S. citizen. Accountants can only work with the numbers that they are given. Accountants are often too busy to remind you to file tax forms. They certainly don't follow you around every day and make notes about your intentions to spend your money. So, the bottom line is that your business starts and ends with you.

My advice: Yes, you need professional services to review your numbers for any errors and oversights and keep within the constantly changing tax laws. But, learn how to control your professionals. Control your accountants. Control your lawyers. Control your bank. Stay in control of your business.

Three Financial Tools Used by Businesses, Banks and the Government

There are three basic financial tools used for business decision-making:

- ***Profit and Loss Statement (P&L)*** *tells* **how much** *money you made*
- ***Balance Sheet*** *tells you* **where** *your money is*
- ***Cash Flow Statement*** *tells you* **when** *you can spend it*

Reading Financial Statements

Most small business entrepreneuers who haven't attended business school must rely on monthly P&L statements (and in some cases fortune cookies) to answer their business questions. I often hear comments like "we're ahead of last year at this time" or "our utilities costs are down over last year."

Again, think of all the possible changes that we mentioned earlier that happen to a company in just one year to impact finances, and your P&L statement; the social, technological, economic environmental, political, legal system, ethical, and demographic changes in age, education and income. This is well worth repeating.

Now add to these, the changes in personnel, and the ownership changes within your customers' and your suppliers' businesses, and even the possible changes in your own business, not to mention the priority changes that show up in your personal life. What possible relevance does a comparison to the previous year have? Yep, you got it. There is no point whatsoever in comparing one year to another. Don't waste your energy chasing ghosts. Focus on the now, 30 days at a time.

Recently, there was a business guru as a guest and speaker on a national television show who claimed that a small business should focus on its balance sheet, not on its sales. His presentation was well received by the audience.

Yes, the speaker is generally correct about keeping an eye on the balance sheet; what you own and what you owe. However, it would be like a medical doctor who is prescribing an aspirin for cancer.

A balance sheet is the <u>result</u> of good financial management. In my opinion, a balance sheet is not a critical component of everyday business decision-making. The person who focuses on a balance sheet would have a different agenda than the day-to-day management of a business. Balance sheet information is needed to get a loan, or for selling or leasing the company, and making purchases that strengthen the company's value. If you are in the start-up phase of your business, don't waste your time right now on balance sheets. You must first get your expenses under control.

To review:

The P&L statement is a list of income and expenses that tells the government how much tax you should pay.

The Balance Sheet is your Kodak moment, your "snapshot-in-time" that tells you where your money is at any point in time.

The Cash Flow statement tells you when you can spend it.

Accurate day-to-day budget management will help you to control the outcome of your balance sheet and your cash flow statement, but not the other way around. Your ability to adhere to a budget is the most important thing you can do for your business. The trick is to get a workable budget in the first place. I say, get some sleep, lower your stress level and watch your headache disappear. Take an aspirin to tie you over until bedtime.

When Are You No Longer A Startup?

An annual revenue of $50,000 or less is considered a hobby. I say that you aren't a real business until you are consistently selling at least $8,000 a month, $100,000 a year. Less than this is what I call a "Seedling". You have a great idea. You're poking at it. It just hasn't happened yet.

The following page gives a simple example of a GAAP P&L. I choose this example of a Start-Up company because it graphically illustrates how the smallest of Start-Up businesses typically spring out of the gate.

A GAAP Example

In my example here we are seeing a tiny business first moving off the launchpad. Notice the GAAP alphabetical arrangement of expenses.

Alphabet Soup – The GAAP P&L

Larry's Landscaping & Garden Supply
Profit & Loss
October 2011 through September 2012

	Oct '11 - Sep 12
Ordinary Income/Expense	
Income	
Landscaping Services	57,860.36
Markup Income	815.00
Retail Sales	383.03
Service	6,640.00
Total Income	65,698.39
Cost of Goods Sold	
Cost of Goods Sold	4,220.25
Total COGS	4,220.25
Gross Profit	61,478.14
Expense	
Payroll Expenses	37,820.65
Automobile	738.05
Bank Service Charges	73.50
Delivery Fee	15.00
Insurance	1,835.00
Interest Expense	470.91
Job Expenses	2,427.25
Mileage Reimbursement	0.00
Professional Fees	375.00
Rent	2,400.00
Repairs	45.00
Tools and Misc. Equipment	735.00
Uncategorized Expenses	0.00
Utilities	655.55
Total Expense	47,590.91
Net Ordinary Income	13,887.23
Other Income/Expense	
Other Income	
Misc Income	762.50
Interest Income	91.11
Total Other Income	853.61
Net Other Income	853.61
Net Income	**14,740.84**

FIG 1.1

I find that most owners of small companies usually base most of their decisions on three numbers: Sales, Net Profit and Gross Profit, in that order.

The P&L

Typically, owners review their Profit and Loss statements (P&Ls are historical data) by first looking at the Gross Sales for the last month. Next, their eyes anxiously skip to the "bottom line" profit. Finally, they might quickly glance at the Gross Profit.

Gross Sales, Net Profit, Gross Profit, Done.

Profit, profit, profit! The definition of the word "profit" is so often confused and there seems to be as many different definitions of profit as the number of people you ask.

Here's little something to put under your hat until a little later. Contrary to popular belief, Profit **is not** the most important number in your business. One month before Toys R Us filed for bankruptcy, they had the highest profit month in their history. Over $300 million dollars. Profit is important, but not the most important. More on this later.

Now I'm going to give you a new word to add to your financial vocabulary. Kanketa substitutes the word "MARGIN" for Gross Profit.

Here's your first GAAP challenge.

GAAP accounting language might confuse you with terms like Net Ordinary Income, Uncategorized Income, Other Income, Miscellaneous Income, Interest Income, Total Other Income, Net Other Income, and Net Income. Will you pay yourself from any of these?

Notice that Net Ordinary Income is both at the bottom and the top of the P&L.

It's hardly a wonder why Start Ups can't get started, and why 85% small businesses fail in the first five years. They have a confusing point of reference.

Net Profit after all expenses.

There is only place in the entire Kanketa system where the word "Profit" is used: Net Profit after all expenses. In this GAAP P&L example, Larry, the business owner, upon seeing the "bottom line" income, is certainly having a joyful day.

"My P&L shows a profit. Why isn't it in my checking account?"

"Ah … It shows a nice profit" comes Larry's shout of sheer delight. Larry might quickly gloss over the Gross Profit in the process. But he is so relieved with the good bottom line news, that he is all too happy to pay the accountant the $250 for the month before Larry tosses the financial statement into the bottom drawer, never again to be looked at.

With a gleeful heart Larry yells up the stairs to his wife; "Hey Sylvia, we made some money this month. We can buy the boat!" It doesn't take long for Sylvia to reply. "Honey, it's great that we made a good profit, but I hate to tell you that there is only $300 in the business account and we need it for groceries."

Most small companies calculate the success of the game by counting ticket sales. They focus on their P&L profit instead of focusing on improving attendance by using their on-the-field playbook. Smart coaches know that If the proven playbook is observed, ticket sales will follow.

When the profit on the P&L is not in the checkbook, a good coach won't obsess about the uncontrollable factors in the marketplace. They only focus on what can be controlled.

When money for payroll is not in the checkbook,

When money to pay suppliers is not in the checkbook,

When money for expenses to run the business is not in the checkbook,

When the Net Profit showing on the P&L is not in the checkbook,

fix your money management process, and don't lose sleep over how last month's underperformance caused this month's problem.

Q: So… what's the point of P&Ls?

A: Preparing to report taxes that aren't due yet.

If you take a minute to search the web for examples of Profit and Loss statements, you will literally find thousands of every type of P&L in existence. Try www.bing.com. Search for Profit and Loss statement images. There are thousands of business P&Ls to pick through.

As you give attention to the main differences between P&Ls you will notice items listed as Job Costs (Cost of Goods Sold). You will see operating overhead costs of every description. Yet, not one of those thousands of statements remotely identifies, suggests or offers real solutions to the day-to-day problems of a business.

> **GAAP Accounting is for tax paying purposes.**
> **GAAP is not a good day-to-day**
> **decision-making tool for business.**

The Kanketa Balanced Budget is a better way to think about, and to manage your finances. A much better way.

The Kanketa Balanced Budget

I am promoting the concept of a Balanced Budget. A Balanced Budget will create short and long-term safety for your company during economic swings, as I am about to show you.

> The Kanketa Balanced Budget is a monetary structure
> of **6** critical business performance components
> that apply to every business on the planet.
> A Balanced Budget provides protection
> against unforeseen change.

I hired an outside research firm to use Google, Bing and every search engine and internet tool they could get their hands on, to find anything close to the Balanced Budgeting practices that I will present here. After six straight months, the research yielded no results of any significant value. I invite you to do your own due diligence. Chances are excellent that after your own research you to will be unable to find the concepts of financial balance that you will learn in this book.

Balanced budgeting is held close to the vest and is almost exclusively practiced at the top of large global companies (and even then, not with great efficiency). A Balanced Budget is almost never seen in a company of less than a couple thousand people.

Why is Financial Balance important? A Balanced Budget is what makes big companies big. I know this firsthand. I learned this over decades from the biggest and the best of them. I guarantee that these practices work just as well in small companies of 1 to 30 employees. They worked in mine.

The Value of a Good Accountant

It is important to understand that accountants actually play a big part in balancing budgets. But their best contributions are different than what their GAAP training teaches. Your accountant is not the final word, but if you know exactly what you need and buy that service from your accountant like you buy groceries or the services of a plumber, an electrician, an auto repair specialist, or any service supplier, your accountant can be a significant part of the financial team of your business.

"Why can't my accountant take care of everything?"

Business Advisor or Accountant?

Bad accounting does not necessarily mean a bad accountant. You are giving your accountant your information to organize. This is why you must become a student of your business. After all, it's your business that promises to support your family and carry you for years. At the very least, learn some sound basics.

Stay in control of your money. Don't just blindly hand it all to an accountant or to anyone for any reason and assume that you are in good hands. This isn't an Allstate commercial. Above all, don't rely on your accountant to walk you through life. He can't, and she won't.

Gotham Is Under Attack

Imagine what would happen if all of the villains attacked Gotham City at once.

The police are losing the battle. The city is in complete turmoil. People everywhere are being dropped in vats of green goo and all the banks are being held for ransom by the Joker and the Penguin. Then the searchlight goes up and hovers over the tall buildings, calling on available heroes for help. But, lo and behold, a silhouette of Robin appears. As the crowds of angry people gather outside of the mayor's office demanding answers, the mayor steps forward with an announcement.

"Friends of Gotham, this year, Robin has the contract. He only charges a small monthly retainer and he's been reasonably reliable. 'Seems to always show up on time. His outfits are clean and in good shape. Granted, he doesn't have the Batmobile, but my office was able to get him a great lease deal on a new Toyota Camry. And, hey, we do trust him. He understands the villains' rules and was sufficiently trained to at least scale the main walls of the important buildings around town. He has good English, keeps good records, and I'm sure he can represent us well to the Joker."

Batman (strategy)	**Robin** (tactics)
BUSINESS FINANCIAL ADVISOR vs.	**ACCOUNTANT**
THE FUNNEL	THE SPOUT
BIG PICTURE	DETAILS
THE SHOE...	... THE LACES
MAIN CATEGORIES	SUB-CATEGORIES
THE SICKLE	THE TRIMMER
BIG SWIPES	CLEAN AND TIDY UP
CREATES BALANCE	MAINTAINS BALANCE
DESIGNS, DEVELOPS	IMPLEMENTS, MANAGES
PROACTIVE	AVOIDS REACTIVE
30 DAY RESULTS	QUARTERLY RESULTS
LEADS IN – Front End	CLOSES OFF – Back End
QUANTIFIES the RESULTS	VERIFIES the OUTCOME
BUDGET, SCORECARD	P&L, BALANCE SHEET

If you want your business to be more than a hobby, you will need both. On rare occasion they come as a two-in-one package, although this is a very uncommon find. I don't recommend it. Both have entirely different training, experiences, and agendas, and almost always, one will outshine the other.

If your goal is balance, then find yourself a great Batman and a great Robin and create balance between them.

Get control of your business, or someone else will; your bank, your creditors, your customers, your suppliers, or maybe even your employees.

True Story: "My Accountant Takes Care of Everything"

Barry F. of Scranton, Pennsylvania was happy with his accounting services. He declined to consider business advisors. After all, his accountant took care of everything – balanced the books, saved the receipts, organized the tax records – the whole shebang. This allowed Barry to focus on his tool and die shop worry free. His accountant took care of everything. All the books, all the receipts, all the taxes. Barry was in very good hands.

One day, Barry received a distressing call that his accountant just passed away.

Barry, who hadn't looked at his books for five years, had no idea where to begin. He knew he needed to find any accountant fast. Despite an exhaustive search, Barry was unable to find an accountant with the same dedication and total service. In despair, Barry began to tackle the books himself.

Barry used his QuickBooks as his bible. His problems grew in proportion to the bookkeeping entry errors he made. He treated whatever ended up at the bottom line of his financial statement as his checkbook balance. Barry spent profits that didn't exist. He managed to keep a shoebox full of receipts, many of which were non-deductible.

It wasn't long before Barry's checkbook was completely empty, and so was his shop. No employees. No equipment. At least there were no more tool and die worries at his new job at UPS.

> The job of a Business Advisor is to help <u>design</u> and <u>develop</u> the big picture and create balance in the business.
> The job of an accountant is to help <u>manage</u> the details and <u>maintain</u> the
> business balance.
> Highly successful businesses have both.

SAFETY BEGINS WITH A BALANCED BUDGET

Your financial journey must follow the road in a specific sequence of events. If you travel on a train, and it makes a 10-minute station stop, you can't wander off to sniff the buttercups in the meadow or you might not get back to the train in time.

As you pack for your trip, begin with the end in mind. If you don't know where you're going, any road will take you there. Your Balanced Budget promises a safe, comfortable ride to the financial destination of your choice.

Unlike the GAAP system that treats all businesses the same, the Balanced Budget is tailored to the size and movement of your business. The route is clearly marked along the way and the Balanced Budget will only produce results that you can handle in proportion to the size of your business.

In Kanketa, Amazon, Google, McDonalds, Coca Cola, will get the exact same results as Larry's Landscaping & Garden Supply, and as it will for your business. The only difference is the relative business size.

> **An efficient business is managed 30 days at a time. Last month was history. Next month hasn't happened yet. In the current 30 days, you either made or lost money. Repeat 12 times in a row for the annual result**

CHAPTER 2

FOLLOW THE MONEY

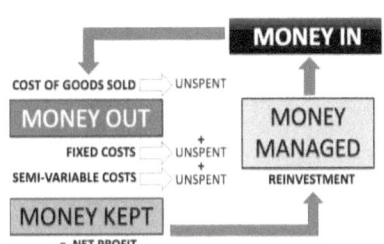

You can't lead your company from behind. Following your budget will keep you on course and ensure that your money arrives at your destination on time. Your 30-Day budget is a straightforward set of instructions, created by folks who have made the trip before.

You and I will establish a specific starting point, a "snapshot in time." Your financial journey begins at midnight on the first day of every month. Your arrival time is scheduled for midnight on the last day of the month. You will either win, or you will lose.

As with any map, you will encounter cracks in the road and detours. You will travel over hills, plains and valleys. There will be caution signs and stop signs to observe that will slow you down and keep you safe. Your money landscape has four connecting lanes that must be managed:

MONEY IN

MONEY OUT

MONEY KEPT

MONEY MANAGED

Wash. Rinse. Repeat.

SIX PARTS OF YOUR KANKETA BALANCED BUDGET

Your balanced budget has six touch points. This is your new Kanketa money language.

MONEY IN (Revenue)

1. GROSS SALES

COST OF QUALITY

2. NET SALES

3. COST OF GOODS SOLD

MONEY OUT (Margin)

4. FIXED COSTS

5. SEMI-VARIABLE COSTS

MONEY KEPT

6. NET PROFIT

MONEY MANAGED

The goal is to create balance within these categories.

"How does this apply to me if I'm just a company of one?"

" Sure, I would like to grow my business, and maybe have an employee or two at some point. But this is a lot of work for little old me. I'm still at the starting gate."

Believe me when I say that if you plan to be a company of one, you will have a job, not a company. No one will buy it for a lot of money or lease it from you later on because there is nothing to buy or lease.

One is the loneliest number

You might be old enough to remember the hit song by the band Three Dog Night, "One is the loneliest number (that ya' ever knew)." As single business owner you are probably doing all the marketing, selling, conducting all customer service and being sure that customers don't leave you. When you are not doing these things, you are creating products and designing services, dealing with suppliers, attending to operational responsibilities and doing bookkeeping.

The output of a business is in direct proportion to the number of managers available. In a company of two people, the workload is cut in half. What doesn't go away are the eight equal and inseparable functions that are required for every company on earth:

Product Management, Production, Delivery, Human Resource Development, Marketing, Sales, Customer Service, and Customer Care.

None of these functions can be ignored to avoid your business from being out of balance and crippled.

All Kanketa practices universally apply to any business size or type. A company of one, or a company of 100,000. The difference isn't the size of the business, but the size of the owner's desire to grow, and their willingness to make change. A Kanketa Balanced Budget does not require a business to be a certain size, or to be in full bloom in order to realize the benefits. The only requirement is that whoever is leading the company must have the desire to grow the business, be willing at any point to make the necessary changes and be diligent about managing money for at least two hours a month.

True Story: A Company of One

Libby H. in Austin, Texas was the sole proprietor of a dog kennel business.

For 12 years, she earned a reasonable living and paid her bills on time. When her mother became ill, Libby closed her kennel to give her mother full time home care.

In choosing to provide home care, Libby fulfilled her role as a devoted daughter.

Unfortunately, Libby didn't realize that keeping her business running and caring for her mother wasn't a binary choice. With just one or two employees and a system that could run the company in her absence, Libby would have received a full time income while taking care of her mother, and she would have been able to return to work at some point in the future while the business continued to grow without her.

I calculated that Libby lost $372,000 by assuming that her company of one was only as big as her mind's eye. The moral of the story: Don't make assumptions about the value of your business based on what you hear from others or what might seem to be the obvious decisions to make. It costs nothing to ask.

Your findings might surprise you.

FINANCIAL BALANCE

THE BALANCING ACT

The Kanketa Balanced Budget is dynamic, holistic, and leaves nothing out. It is often called a "transitional budget" because the expenses and the Net Profit move and breathe in balance with the sales performance of the business.

There are two factors that should always be considered with every business decision you make:

- *Financial Balance is essential to building stability, safety and growth.*
- *The impact of every decision you make will bring you closer to or drive you away from a point of balance.*

Kanketa defines Financial Balance as...

> the relationship of Fixed overhead costs
> that do not change from month to month,
> to Semi-Variable overhead costs,
> that do change from month to month.
>
> to safely produce the most net profit possible
> without damaging the business.

"UUUgh. That's a mouthful. I don't get it."

Not yet. But you will. This is what you will learn in this book. I understand exactly where you are right now. I was there many more than a dozen times in my life.

WHAT IS "NORMAL"?

"Normal" is a financial performance term that will be used with great regularity.

Normal is the ideal monthly sales performance level at which all resources are fully utilized without the need for further expense. Normal is the starting point for the growth of a business.

When you are assembling your budget, do not guess. The best source of Normal numbers are the past 12 calendar months of sales and expense performance. It shows your business seasonality, the ups and the downs. Use last year's P&L. Be sure to consider your budget from all angles.

Be **S** PECIFIC	Have a specific sales target amount. "Based on last year, I think we can sell $720,000 again. That's our $60,000 a month."
Be **M** EASURABLE	"We will track monthly goals and measure against quarterly goals."
Be **A** CHIEVABLE	"We have enough people to do the work. There is enough workspace, supplies, suppliers, Line of Credit to produce this."
Be **R** EASONABLE	"We could easily double this sales target, but based on my personal priorities of wanting to travel four months out of the year, and working part time while managing the kids and with mom in Assisted Living, I will be happy to achieve last year's sales."
Be **T** IMELY	We will set sales benchmarks with given dates to accomplish them.

I often hear "last year was different". There was COVID19. There was a fire in the plant. I was laid up for 2 months. My friend, the world is constantly adjusting. You will always have some reason to think that last year was out of the ordinary. Please use last year's P&L for this process. They are the best numbers available. Once your Balanced Budget is set up, it will self-adjust.

Last year's performance is this year's NORMAL.

MONEY IN

All the money that

hits your business checkbook

CHAPTER 3

BUDGET PART 1 OF 6
GROSS SALES

The demand for your products
and services

Gross Revenue
minus all the money that is not from your customers
for the sale of Products and Services
= your Gross Sales

We begin with the money coming in the door. Kanketa defines Gross Sales as the total amount of money that is <u>deposited</u> into your bank as a result of the sale and/or production of your products and services.

Just because you deposited money into your business checkbook, doesn't necessarily mean that it is MONEY IN to your business.

Gross Revenue

After many years of working with thousands of small businesses, I continue to witness general misconceptions about "Gross Sales".

You would think that Gross Sales is an accepted standard definition. After all, aren't Gross Sales all the money that comes into the company?

Not always. In small businesses, Gross Sales are often mingled with general bank deposits - "miscellaneous income." Refunds, loans to the business, credits, loan payments from friends, etc. When you can't specifically identify money coming into your business, your accountant will label it "Uncategorized Income" and keep moving. You need to take time to properly label every penny coming into your business. Guesswork will drive accountants cuckoo.

In GAAP, you will hear the terms, "cash accounting method" and "accrual accounting method".

Accrual Accounting
In businesses selling to businesses (B2B), "Accrual" is the accumulation of payments owed to you by your customer for work that you have completed but have not yet invoiced to your customer. Accrual is an accounting method that records your sales revenues and expenses as you complete the various portions of a job regardless of when you are paid. An invoice is a statement of the money due for your agreed-to products and services; a bill.

Cash Accounting
Cash accounting is an accounting method under which revenue is recognized when cash is received, and expenses are recognized when cash is paid. Most retail businesses use cash accounting at the register.

Kanketa recommends that your business uses a cash accounting system no matter what type of business you have.

True Story: Count Sales, Not Revenue

For years, Steve H. of Noblesville, Indiana ran a respectable auto repair business. He was passionate about his work and treated his employees well. Steve loved cars and spent most of his time under the hood. Steve didn't take to bookkeeping, and he didn't trust others to manage his money. He did as little as possible to manage his banking affairs, other than making deposits and signing checks.

Steve started his business without bank loans. Instead, he took loans from friends and family. In the early 1990's, Steve's business began to grow, and along with it, so did his banking duties. Customer payments were coming in faster than ever, and Steve found himself depositing money every other day.

Steve had a habit of mixing customer payments with loans from friends and family, refund from vendors, credits for product returns and whatever hit the bank. Then, at the end of the month when things slowed down a bit, Steve would glance at his bank statements and, low and behold, marvel at all the deposits, which to Steve, were his total sales for the month. Every so often I heard Steve say: "Ooops, yeah, I forgot that Phil paid me a refund." Not only was this a nightmare for Steve's accountant, but these casual habits continued for years. Steve would boast that his shop was doing $500,000 a year, when, in reality he was only selling 80% of this amount.

Finally, Steve went to get a business loan for expansion. On the application, where it asks, "What are your annual sales?" Steve proudly entered a half million dollars. The bank's underwriters begged to differ because Steve's cashflow only supported a company with $410,000 Gross Sales. Steve was very disappointed with what the bank would lend him.

Fast forward seven years, Steve decided to sell his company. There were several interested buyers. When their accountants poured over Steve's financials, they soon learned that Steve's sales performance was not as represented. The highest bidder was only willing to pay less than half of the asking price for the business.

After removing all the irrelevant, miscellaneous income in the audit, Steve hobbled away with a disappointing settlement for far less money than he thought his business was worth.

All too often, small business managers and owners fail to take the time to clearly, accurately and properly identify and separate their general incoming payments from their sales activity. Many small companies routinely accept and deposit various types of revenue into one general business checking account without properly separating and logging the deposit information.

There are many reasons why deposits might not be sales related. For example: A business loaned money to a key struggling supplier to keep the supplier in business. After they received and deposited the supplier's loan payments, they discovered later that they mistakenly recorded the money as Gross Sales. Also, they might've deposited interest payments from a loan they made into the general checking account. They might have deposited overpayments and reimbursements from vendors. Maybe it's a loan from family and friends. There are many different types of deposits that fall under the title of revenue that aren't a sale from products and services. I will use revenue as a general term for all deposits: cash sales, credit card transactions, outside loan repayments - everything that you are paid!

> **Companies too often deposit various types of revenue into one general checking account without properly identifying the revenue.**

Label it to Enable it!

When someone pays you, the payment falls under the title of general revenue (miscellaneous income) until it is clear that you are paid for a specific product or service that you make and/or sell. Only then can it be counted as a Gross Sale. Still, only you know what the money received was for.

When deposits are not clearly labeled, the total Gross Sales picture becomes cloudy, and the important financial details can be inaccurate. It is critical to specifically notate the purpose of every deposit. A casually scribbled memo or a missing notation can lead to misinterpretation.

Account Codes

At one point, someone came up with the idea of labeling all the aspects of profit and loss with a set of numbers called "account codes." Using these account codes will reduce confusion.

By the way, everything here might seem like it's specifically aimed at manufacturing. It isn't. Please know that everything here equally applies to any service or non-profit business.

It is my experience that small businesses rely too heavily on their accountants to categorize and classify their income and expenses. Your accountant isn't following you around every day. S/he can't sniff out your intentions for your income and expenses. Without complete information about your company's finances, your accountant must do guesswork to make sense of things. The guesses can be wrong and cost you a lot of money. Failure to provide your accountant with timely, accurate, legible, and complete information can get expensive and lead to unnecessary errors and significant tax expenses.

Why else do you think accountants have those long legal disclaimers on the first page of your financial statements? They are disclaiming their guesses. The bottom line: use your account codes.

THE SALE: TO BE OR NOT TO BE

What is a "Sale"?

The variety of answers cause large misunderstandings daily in the world's largest of companies. Just because you send someone an invoice, does not necessarily mean that you made a sale.

... A Target

A sale includes a legal agreement to provide a clearly defined value, or a set of deliverables within a specific timeframe, for a specific payment amount.

... A Budget

The payment may be an agreed to amount or "payment in kind", whether the payment is in exchange for things like a trade for services or tangible items, service time, or any other form of equal value. Barter requires the same documentation as cash.

... A Timeframe

A sale must be delivered within a specified time to keep the contract legal.

> **In Kanketa, a sale must be fully earned, and is only final when the payment is available to spend and there is nothing more to deliver and no further liability.**

Gross Revenue is Not Necessarily Gross Sales

Gross Revenue of products and services is all deposits into the company checkbook; sales revenue, loans, interest revenue, warranty revenue, factoring revenue, etc. However, Gross Revenue does not necessarily specify which money you deposit comes from the sales of your products and services. As memory slips, so does the reason why you were paid. It is crucial to keep income and expenses carefully identified using your account codes.

At the end of the year, you don't want to have a false sense of how your business performed because your product sales were mixed with unrelated income. Imagine how bitterly disappointed you'd feel if you learned that instead of depositing $200,000 from the sales of products and services, you actually only received $130,000 from the products and services you provided.

When used properly, account codes should add definition, organization and clarity to the sources of your income, and help you to separate the purpose of your income and expenses. You may use your accountant's codes or use your own. If your accountant is more comfortable with their account codes, then, by all means use them. The account numbers are not as important as the organizational benefits you get from using codes.

The formal numbering system for all money activity in your business is your "Chart of Accounts."

Account codes will help you to expose, avoid and remove error, and increase your overall financial accuracy. This helps you to keep more money in the short and long run. In the Kanketa system, the Chart of Accounts will be critical to your financial success as you will learn later in this book.

Right of Rescission

A sale produces a payment from a customer that may be on deposit, but technically, the payment should not be spent for 72 hours. This gives your customer the right to inspect the delivery of each portion or all of the completed work before they accept your bill.

This is called a "Right of Rescission."

Work in Progress: Earned Income

By law, you may only spend customer's money up to that portion of the work that has already been satisfactorily completed. Most small business owners believe that they can spend all money as they want for whatever they want when they receive and deposit it – even if it is intended as a pre-payment, advanced for work to be done. This is not legally correct. Many business owners spend money received and intended for one customer to pay for another customer's job. This comingling of funds leaves a grey area for legal dispute – a close cousin to a Ponzi Scheme.

There is a law in most states that protects your customer from "contractor theft," which is a felony punishable by fines and often, jail time. When you accept and spend customer money for a job that is not yet fully completed, you may only spend the customer's money in proportion to the work that is finished, documented and delivered.

If you buy materials and supplies for the job, you may spend that portion of the customer's money for the materials and supplies. If you complete 20% of the work, you may only spend 20% of the customer's payment for service that you furnished or satisfactorily delivered. In all cases, you must be able to produce evidence of completion.

If evidence of any earned income is missing, you have a sale in progress, but you do not legally have a completed sale. Without proof of a specifically defined target, an agreed to monetary exchange or equal value for service and a defined start-end time frame for delivery, chances are excellent that you would lose in a court of law. I've seen cases where the judge demanded to see the supplier's checkbook. The bank balance was lower than the unfinished work that the customer paid for. The supplier was guilty of contractor theft, a felony resulting in restitution and jail time.

When you accept and deposit the customer's payment, <u>spend only that money for which you have evidence of completion</u> and only for the work you have delivered in proportion to the value of all labor, services, products and/or materials. In a job that has several payments, notify the customer in writing of the work that you have completed as you complete it.

Be sure to identify all income and expenses with account codes.

Gross Income (Gross Revenue) is all money that is received during the year.

Earned income is paid for time and includes only wages, commissions, bonuses, and business income, minus expenses, if the person is self-employed.

> You may only spend "earned income" from customer payments that you receive in proportion to the work for which you have evidence of satisfactory completion.

If, by state law, fees are earned for the proportionate amount of a job already done – not for work to be done – you may not spend the money received that is not yet earned. Be sure to be able to show recorded evidence that the work specifically invoiced to a customer was satisfactorily completed. If you have no evidence of completion, it has not been earned, and the invoice that you send does not yet qualify.

True Story: The Missing Four Sentence Email That Cost $30,000

Alex's K's construction company in southern Wisconsin was hired to do a home remodeling project. The total of the project was $95,000. The homeowner paid Alex $65,000 toward the job. A shortage of workers delayed Alex by 3 weeks. In the meantime, Alex spent $30,000 on payroll for other work that his company was able to complete during the delay.

The homeowner decided to halt the project and demanded an immediate full refund of the $65,000. Alex claimed that there was $30,000 in completed work. The homeowner took Alex to Court and sued for the full amount. Since Alex could not produce evidence of "earned income," the judge's ruling was contractor theft by law.

A simple email notification by Alex to the homeowner immediately after the $30,000 of work was completed with a detailed description of the work delivered would have prevented the unfavorable outcome. Regardless of the actual work completed, Alex had to repay the full amount with payments over years to avoid a felony charge.

Suggested Email:

Hello (Mr. Homeowner),

On Tuesday, September 16th, 2018, we completed 15% of your total job. We delivered the list of services shown in the attachment. Please inspect this part of the job. If I have not heard otherwise by September 19th, I will assume that this part of the project was to your complete satisfaction.

Thank you for the opportunity to serve you.

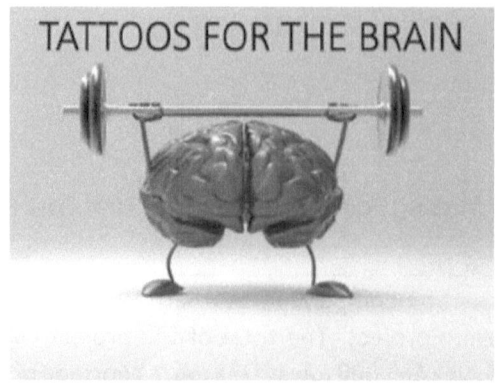

TATTOOS FOR THE BRAIN

THREE GROSS SALE TATTOOS FOR THE BRAIN

Here are three main takeaways for the Gross Sales in a Kanketa Balanced Budget.

#1. A Sale must have a target, a budget (monetary or value exchange) and a specified time frame to be legally collectible.

#2. A Sale has a 72-hour Right of Rescission, an allowed time for the customer to inspect the product or service before using it or officially taking possession of it, unless the customer provides proof of satisfaction and full acceptance before that time.

#3. You may only spend "earned income" from customer payments that you receive in proportion to the work for which you have evidence of satisfactory completion.

CHAPTER 4

BUDGET PART
NET SALES

The Reliable Income of Your Business

Gross Revenue
minus all money that is not from your customers
for the sale of your Products and Services
= Gross Sales
minus Cost of Quality = Net Sales

There are two parts to a sale: Gross Sale and Net Sale. The Gross Sale is the total amount of money that you expect to receive from producing and/or selling your products and services or for other payments you receive for products or services, such as the interest and late fees that you charge.

Cost of Quality, the conditional "**IF THEN**" money

Now comes the "OOPS", the **O**ften-**O**verlooked **P**art of the **S**ale, which is something called the "Cost of Quality." Instinctively, you might feel that Cost of Quality is a MONEY OUT cost. I choose to put it with MONEY IN because you have an opportunity to keep some of it. It's technically not your money in the first place. It's money that the customer is conditionally and temporarily handing over to you and taking back before doing business with you.

"You will get the job **IF** I get a sample first."
"You will get the job **IF** I get a survey first."
"You will get the job **IF** I get a perfect product or service."
"You will get the job **IF** I get a guarantee."
"You will get the job **IF** I can have some money back as a discount."

Every business has a Cost of Quality. It looks like part of the sale. It might hit your checkbook at one point, but it leaves just as quickly.

Returns and Allowances

On your tax return, the IRS recognizes the Cost of Quality as "Returns and Allowances." Kanketa sees returns and allowances as more than a few items that you can deduct from your taxes for returning a product back or writing off an unpaid customer debt.

Cost of Quality is the total money that might or might not be deposited that you don't get to keep… (well, maybe). Most small businesses do not charge for Cost of Quality and owners too often look at Cost of Quality as a cost of doing business. If, however, it is tracked, monitored, managed and charged for like any other business expense, it is now part of MONEY IN – all income of the business.

Cost of Quality includes your customer discounts that you allow, and somehow hope to recapture later.

Cost of Quality is your money for the product and service warranties that you stand by, the money that you receive now but will eventually pay out if customers return defective or underperforming products. Warranties are a liability to your company.

Cost of Quality are the costs of your customer freebies; the cost of your samples, free tests, trials and surveys not charged for to get the customer interested. These expenses evaporate and are generally not recovered unless you make an effort to do so.

Cost of Quality are your discounts to employees for products and services. These are your non-charged cost of production, plus your cost of operating, plus your lost profit (since you could have sold these products to your customers for full price).

Cost of Quality are your returns and rework because of internal errors.

The bottom line: Cost of Quality are the cost of customer discounts, costs for error and rework, defects or a return of a product that was not delivered as expected, warranties that your customer still might redeemed in the future, restocking costs, free samples that you give away, and customer and vendor errors that you can't get paid for.

Cost of Quality is rarely tracked and is often elusive. Cost of Quality only shows up on your P&L when the expenses are identified, tracked and paid out.

Gross Sales are the total collected amount that you invoice before the Cost of Quality (discounts, rework, returns, samples, free assessments, warranties and error). Net Sales are the money you keep after all Costs of Quality have been deducted.

The money left after removing these often overlooked and unaccounted for items is your Net Sale – the money that you get to work with in your business. Net Sales more accurately represent your true sales picture.

Who Pays for Cost of Quality When the Customer Doesn't?

Most small business owners call the Cost of Quality a cost of doing business. They don't invest a lot of time or effort trying to recover these costs in view of everything else that needs to be accomplished.

The Kanketa philosophy is you don't always have to win, just never lose. Kanketa sees every loss as critical, regardless of its size. Tiny leaks lead to small losses, lead to bigger losses. Loss is not classified in order of importance. Loss is loss.

The Kanketa system recommends budgeting, tracking, monitoring and eventually recovering Cost of Quality. These costs should be built into the price as part of the company's service. If these costs are not recovered, the owner of the business personally pays for Cost of Quality out of the owner's Net Profit.

Why Track Cost of Quality?

The Kanketa system tracks the Cost of Quality to get to the Net Sale. Net Sales more accurately represent your true sales picture. In some businesses, Cost of Quality can be a big number. It can also get out of control quite easily.

The Net Sale is the actual money you keep after subtracting your Cost of Quality from your Gross Sale. This is the total amount of money that you have to work with for the job.

I use a "recovery bank" that reminds me to tag Cost of Quality recovery charges and build them into future sales.

I encourage you to clearly define and closely monitor your Cost of Quality and develop a recovery process that is comfortable for you. In any regard, you should always budget something for Cost of Quality. If Cost of Quality includes the cost of errors made by your company that you must write checks for, then, certainly you are on a mission to avoid and eliminate error. This is all the more reason why it is valuable to monitor, measure and track Cost of Quality.

> **Net Sales, after deducting Cost of Quality, is the amount of money with which the month's budget is established.**

True Story: Discounts Are Paid for By the Owner

Phillip T's Bar-B-Que restaurant in Boston gave discounts to every customer to entice them to return. Phillip allowed 17 employees to eat at half-price. His cooks often made significant kitchen errors. Yet, Phillip freely gave out promotional coupons for every holiday and occasion. He gave generous discounts to the police and government workers. He was more than happy to give discounts to veterans, and to most charity organizations.

Phillip had excellent food, and his revenue grew briskly every year by nearly 30%. Three years later, after his sales had more than doubled, Phillip found himself working harder, and longer to earn the same salary while his company profits steadily dwindled.

Phillip's food was in demand, but his high Cost of Quality had equaled his Net Profit. He found himself working overtime to keep up with his discounts.

Finally, Phillip had to close his doors because he couldn't meet expenses. Phillip's unattended Cost of Quality ate his company for lunch.

> **Discounts and rebates must be planned for and budgeted. If you don't do this, you are expecting the owner to pay for them out of the owner's pocket.**

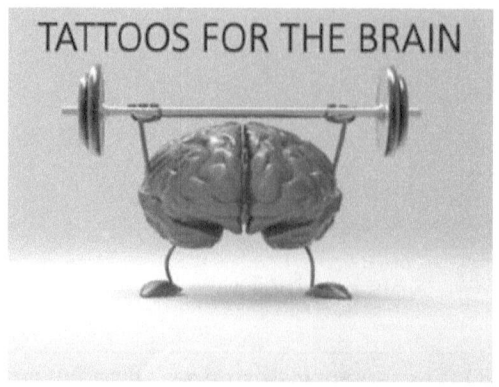

THREE NET SALE TATTOOS FOR THE BRAIN

Here are three main takeaways for the Net Sales of a Kanketa Balanced Budget.

#1. A Net Sale is the amount of money you have to work with after discounts, returns, allowances and error.

#2. A Net sale, not a Gross Sale, is the primary income number that is used to determine the performance of a business.

#3. A Net Sale is the result of total deposits for products and services, minus the Cost of Quality. The Cost of Quality should be monitored, tracked and be ultimately recoverable in the price of the products and services.

CHAPTER 5

BUDGET PART 3 OF 6
COST OF GOODS SOLD

The job costs to produce your products
and services

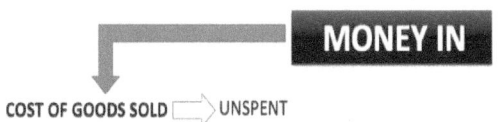

**Gross Revenue
minus all money that is not from your customers
for the sale of products and services = Gross Sales
minus Cost of Quality = Net Sales
minus Cost of Goods Sold
= the money that you keep for overhead to operate the company
and make a profit**

If you don't have a job, you don't have Cost of Goods Sold.

Job related costs are also known as Cost of Goods Sold. Accountants will sometimes refer to Cost of Goods as "Cost of Sales." You don't have job costs (Cost of Goods Sold) unless or until you have a job. This makes your job costs dynamic; they are "variable costs" because they vary with the performance of your business.

Every business has at least 20% Cost of Goods Sold buried somewhere. When I ask an attorney what their Cost of Goods Sold are, I get "Oh, it's just me. My consulting time. I might buy a few supplies to do a job, and maybe some court fees.... so, I'd say 10% at the most."

"Oh, really? Do you ever contract to paralegals?"

"Well, yeah.... sometimes."

"That's a Cost of Goods Sold".

"Do you ever give a case to another attorney because you are overloaded, and you bill the client but put a markup in for yourself?"

"All the time."

"That's a Cost of Goods Sold".

"Do you spend for courier services?"

"Routinely."

"That's Cost of Goods Sold".

"Would you say then, that a more accurate Cost of Goods Sold budget would be closer to 40% of your practice, and this is why you charge $250 an hour?"

"'Gee... guess so."

Attorneys, like every other small business, can and do go bankrupt for the exact same reasons.

Every job-related cost is a variable Cost of Goods Sold. You only have the costs if you have a job.

I used to do a fun little exercise while I was driving to a customer. I'd look around at businesses and see if I could identify their Cost of Goods Sold.

A Bank? Part of the Cost of Goods Sold is the money that they buy and sell at a profit.

A Pet Store? Part of the Cost of Goods Sold is the money is the cost to clean up a pet and make it ready for sale.

Get the picture?

Cost of Goods Sold are classified under five general headings:

COST OF GOODS SOLD

1.	**Direct Outside labor**	Individual 1099 workers by the job
2.	**Commissions**	Outside compensation to find and/or sell
3.	**Contracted services**	Companies by the job
4.	**Materials and supplies**	Raw Materials. Brokered Products and Services
5.	**A category for "all other"**	

All job-related expensess

Rentals

Licenses and Permits required

Transportation – People

Shipping Materials and Supplies

Etc.

ALSO INCLUDED:

Advertising or promotion – but only as it relates to a specific product or service

Sales tax (*You only have it if you make a sale. You don't have it if you don't make a sale*)

Kanketa loves round numbers in budgets. Kanketa hates round numbers in accounting.

Cost of Goods Sold are needed to create and produce your products and services. Trying to count, track, remember and manage budget numbers that you have little control over is a waste of time.

It's a good idea to keep your Cost of Goods budget as a rounded, easy number to remember.

When your business performs at 100% Normal, the budget at 100% should only reflect the Cost of Goods Sold required to produce the Normal sales level. Nothing more. Nothing less. In other words, at 100% Normal performance, the business should never need more Cost of Goods Sold to achieve that level of delivery, whatever "that" is.

By ensuring this, the Cost of Goods Sold percent should follow in proportion to Gross Sales performance at any sales level.

If your month-to-month Cost of Goods Sold expenses aren't proportionate in percent to your Gross Sales, either your Normal budget is incorrectly budgeted, or you need to improve how you manage these costs.

COST OF GOODS SOLD IN PROPORTION TO
DIFFERENT NET SALES LEVELS

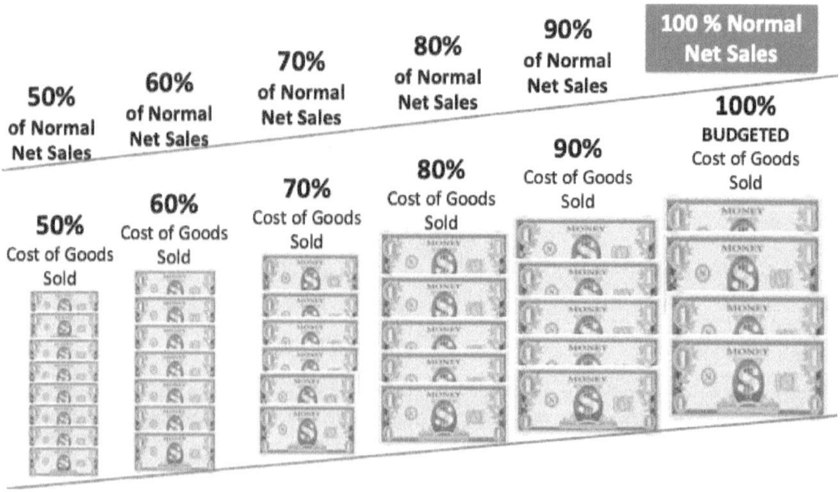

FIG 5.1

Cost of Goods Sold: Emotion Over Logic

The Cost of Goods Sold are typically managed reactively. Job costs in small companies are often created and paid for out of emotion, rather than logic. The least restraint is placed on paying those suppliers who are calling every day and demanding payments, while the most lucrative customers are constantly screaming at and badgering the business to deliver the products they expect.

Cost of Goods bills can be paid any time in the month. However, a policy of paying half the month's job costs by the middle of the month, and the other half at the end of the month helps to control cash flow and gives you time to think.

Paying less often, and more deliberately gives you that much needed extra time to assess and evaluate your decisions about your supply expenses and your supplier value. Did your suppliers deliver on their promises and give you what you bargained for on target, on budget, on time? If not, why not?

Slowing down your supplier payments, tightening up your policies, and keeping to fewer pay days is highly recommended. This control is vital to better overall cost planning.

Who Owns Your Business? You... or Your Suppliers?

And now, a word about suppliers. Here's the Kanketa 50% rule about controlling your business.

We live in an interdependent world. Suppliers are always tossing in conveniences to drive up the sale. They can quite easily take over your business if you aren't careful. Your strategic suppliers are those who have your best interest in mind. They are the ones who work at being good suppliers and who make a real effort to understand your vision and mission and your ups and downs. They want to win but want you to win as well. They are your long-term, most trusted partners who will gladly work with you on your payment terms. Your fewer, better strategic suppliers should get most of the work.

I've generally used a rule of thumb that the percentage of my Cost of Goods Sold to my Gross Sales is a factor of my overall business safety.

"How much should my Cost of Goods Sold be?"

I am safe when my Cost of Goods Sold is less than 50% of my Gross Sales. I am not as concerned about a single vendor holding me up on their terms. I am less safe when my Cost of Goods Sold is more than 50% of my Gross Sales. If I am a distributor with Cost of Goods being 60%, I am 10% less safe (50% safe Cost of Goods Sold level minus my 10% risk factor). If my Cost of Goods is 70%, I am 20% less safe.

NOTE: Some businesses, by their very nature, such as a bank, insurance broker, commodity or food broker, etc. are not in a position to achieve anything near a 50% level for Cost of Goods Sold. However, they are typically businesses that are relied upon by entire industries such as wholesalers, and distributors. Their safety is strictly in volume sales to many, many accounts. Let's assume that you are not in the commodity category.

For a host of reasons your suppliers could change policy on a dime, merge or get sold, and you'd have to bow to their whims or give way to an uncontrollable industry movement.

Stay always vigilant about this balance. Any change can quickly and unexpectedly cause your suppliers to control you. Change management should be part of your strategy and everyday management routine. Safety first. Profit Second.

If you are selling a product or service with a high Cost of Goods Sold, continue to look for other products and add them to your mix to bring your Cost of Goods Sold into a total balance with your margin of 50% or less.

> **If you don't have a job, you don't have Cost of Goods Sold. Your percentage of Cost of Goods Sold to Gross Sales is a safety factor. The lower the Cost of Goods percent of Gross Sales, the higher the percentage of business safety.**

True Story: The Case for Fewer, Better Supplier Relationships

---

Tyler T, of Omaha, Nebraska had an electronics shop that sold cameras, lighting and security devices. Tyler never paid his suppliers on time or treated them properly. He would run up bills as far as they allowed him to and when they started to pressure him for payment, he would take his business to the next supplier.

This continued for quite a while. Tyler was severely in debt, and had taken advantage of all his key suppliers, but he didn't seem to care. His attitude was, "there's plenty more where that came from".

One day an industry manufacturer unexpectedly introduced a new technology for a unique self-charging battery, allowing its devices an additional two hours of emergency use before replacement. The key suppliers who Tyler mistreated were awarded exclusive distributorships. No one would sell to Tyler.

Needless to say, Tyler's business closed.

It's one thing to run into debt. It's harder to run into the suppliers. Key suppliers who are willing to stand by you and understand and work with you are the lifeblood of a business. Those who value accountability and integrity, show respect through open, honest communication and seek collaborative problem-solving, will build sustainable businesses.

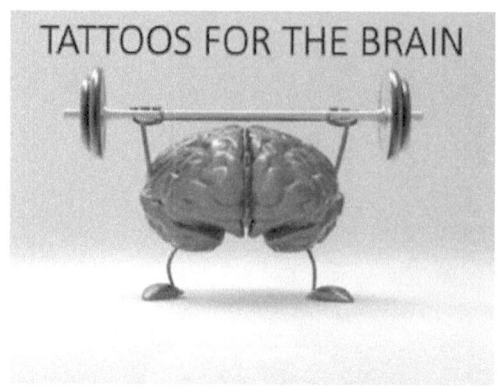

TATTOOS FOR THE BRAIN

THREE COST OF GOODS SOLD TATTOOS FOR THE BRAIN

Here are three main takeaways for the Cost of Goods Sold of a Kanketa Balanced Budget.

#1. Nothing is a Cost of Goods Sold unless there is a customer that buys it and there is a verifiable job. No job? No Cost of Goods Sold.

#2. The lower the Cost of Goods Sold percent to Gross Sales, the higher the percentage of business safety that exists.

#3. The goal of Cost of Goods Sold is to balance like-product types so that the overall percentage of Cost of Goods Sold to Net Sales is relatively constant from year to year.

MONEY OUT

All the money that

it costs to operate

your company

CHAPTER 6

MONEY OUT

THE MARGIN
(The Operating Costs
of your Business)

The Only Meaningful Business Growth

Spend only what you can afford by keeping your Margin in balance.

Gross Sales minus Cost of Quality = Net Sales
Net Sales minus Cost of Goods Sold = Margin
Margin is another word for Gross Profit.

If you were to ask 100 people how profitable their companies are, you are likely to get 100 different answers. For this reason, Kanketa avoids the confusion of the word "Gross Profit," and instead, calls it "Margin" (the money left after subtracting Cost of Goods Sold from Net Sales).

As you might have suspected by now, the Kanketa system has its own language. Earlier, we defined Normal as the ideal monthly sales performance level at which all resources are fully utilized without the need for further expense.

"Normal Monthly Margin" will be used throughout this book. Every number in your budget is calculated from Normal. The Normal Monthly Margin (an ideal month) is the money left every month after you remove Cost of Goods Sold and Cost of Quality at 100% "Normal" sales levels.

Margin is the only money that counts when you talk about company growth.

In Kanketa, your **ideal** Margin is the Normal Margin.

Your Normal Balanced Margin has 2 equal parts, and their sub-parts

FIXED COSTS DO NOT CHANGE SIGNIFICANTLY FROM MONTH TO MONTH

> **FIXED PEOPLE COSTS** (repeatable month to month manager's salaries)

> **FIXED "NON-PEOPLE" COSTS** - not a person (month-to-month, predictably repeatable overhead expenses necessary to maintain your business performance and profitability. All overhead costs that aren't manager salaries)

SEMI-VARIABLE COSTS DO CHANGE FROM MONTH TO MONTH

> **SEMI-VARIABLE PEOPLE COSTS** (managers' pay that changes with company performance)

> **SEMI-VARIABLE NON-PEOPLE COSTS**, not a person (changing monthly overhead expenses necessary to grow your business and increase your profitability)

When all these components are equal, you have a Balanced Budget.

Margin pays for all company overhead; the total costs required to operate the business every day, every month of every year, whether you have $1 of sales, or $1 million in sales. Operating costs pay for managers and Non-People Costs which are everything that is not a person, such as rent, utilities, phones, insurance, etc., as well as a Net Profit for the owner.

Some people incorrectly refer to Margin as "Net Income". More accurately, Net Income is the amount of money that is left after all the company's debts and expenses are subtracted from all its total income.

It's hardly a wonder why small business owners struggle with finance. There is a tremendous disconnect about the use of financial terms and their meanings.

WHAT IS BUSINESS GROWTH?

"Is my business growing, or just going?"

Margin isn't everything. It's the only thing.

What would you say if someone told you that they can guarantee to double your revenue in two years? You'd probably feel pretty good, wouldn't you? Overjoyed would be a better word. After all, the company's profit has slipped a bit and doubling the revenue is going to really take care of things.

SALES

Year. 1	Year. 2	Year. 3
$ 1 million	$ 2 million	$ 3 million

FIG 6.1

Some companies believe that more sales will make up for shrinking Net Profit. This is unsustainable, and an extremely risky assumption that will, more often than not, bankrupt you.

	Year. 1	Year. 2	Year. 3
	$ 1 million	$ 2 million	$ 3 million
SALES MARGIN	$ 500k	$ 400k	$ 300k
PROFIT	$ 165k	$ 130k	$ 100k

FIG 6.2

Here you see that doubled revenue has nothing to do with Net Profit. It is truly ironic that all those large global companies that go bankrupt have floors of high-paid, six-figure accounting wizards from the top business schools in the country on their payroll.

When a company makes a significant reinvestment to generate more sales in hopes of making up for shrinking Net Profit, it is taking its eyes off the ball.

So, why the bankruptcies when they can afford the best and most brilliant minds in the world? Perhaps, those six-figure accountants have the right ladder leaning against the wrong wall. They were using ticket sales to make decisions on the field, when all along they needed a playbook.

Declining sales makes most investors very nervous. Some companies had smart, experienced leadership who know the difference between variable, direct and indirect costs. They focused on Margins.

SALES

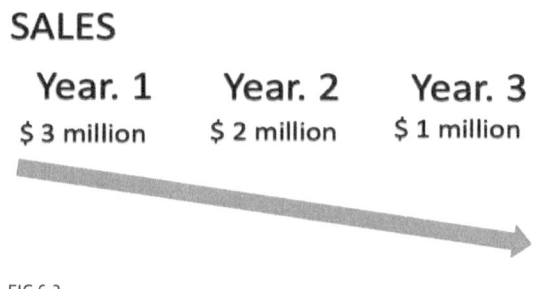

Year. 1	Year. 2	Year. 3
$ 3 million	$ 2 million	$ 1 million

FIG 6.3

2006: STARBUCKS

Take Starbucks for instance. Starbucks made big leaps quickly out of the gate, spending much of its profit trying to become the leader in the coffee market. Starbucks over-expanded, diluting profits and damaging the brand (not every corner needed a Starbucks). By 2006 net income had fallen dramatically, cutting the stock price in half.

Margin Increase

In 2008, after some revealing research, the Starbuck leaders found that they weren't really in the coffee business at all. They were in the neighborhood meeting place business, that just happened to sell good coffee.

Starbucks repackaged itself as a business meeting place with a whole new approach. The company was able to turn things around despite slipping sales. With a narrow concentration on service, the company restructured its supply costs and pricing, improved operational efficiency and incrementally and carefully expanded its product offerings. The company not only recovered but grew far beyond expectations. The rest is history.

Starbucks wasn't the only one that responded wisely to its marketing problems.

McDonald's removed Ronald as its main character and began to concentrate on healthier food for the whole family. Coca-Cola competed against itself by buying up the competition. Apple computer reinvented its product line and diversified by adding Apple TV, steamy streaming video games, Apple iPad, Apple iPhone, Apple iTunes and many more. Marvel Comic Books marched head on into the movie business. Pabst Blue Ribbon went into the licensing business. Swatch attached the jewelry market and became more than a watch. Others followed. By focusing on Margin and the root causes of the low Margin problems, these companies alone rescued an estimated 3.2 million jobs.

This example shows how declining sales is not necessarily the whole picture.

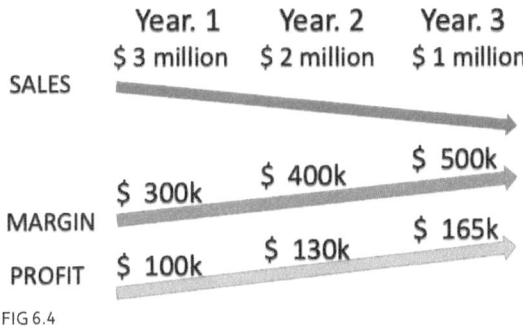

FIG 6.4

Two Myths That Kill Small Companies

There are hundreds of stories that all lead to the same bad place because of two deadly business myths ...

Myth #1: More sales is meaningful growth.

Fact: More sales does not necessarily reflect growth, and if not controlled, could severely damage a business and even put it into bankruptcy (Toys-R-Us, and a legion of others).

Myth #2: More loans and more funding will correct the problem.

Fact: Debt does not create growth unless it has a specific return on investment of 3X the face amount.

There is nothing wrong with controlled business debt as long as the purpose of the loan ultimately causes the debt to be eliminated. A loan that does not produce at least three times return on investment can make a bigger problem than if you never borrowed the money at all.

Margin Growth is the Only Meaningful Growth

The single most important idea that I want to convey in this section is that Margin growth is the only meaningful growth in your company. Grow your Margin and you'll grow your company. Growing sales without growing Margin mathematically creates a predictable result: bankruptcy. This is how it all ties together.

> **Margin isn't everything. It's the only thing. Margin, not Gross Sales, determines the real growth of the business.**

MARGIN EXPENSES:
FIXED COSTS AND SEMI-VARIABLE COSTS

Gross Sales minus Cost of Quality = Net Sales
Net Sales minus Cost of Goods Sold = Margin
Margin = Fixed Costs and Semi-Variable Costs
to operate the business.

In the Margin two types of costs must be in balance to keep the business from falling... but they are not necessarily equal in size or type.

Net Profit is the fulcrum.

Equal, but Not in Balance?

Balance refers to orderly movement, an even distribution of weight enabling someone or something to remain upright and steady. Balance is a condition in which different elements are in correct proportions.

Correctly Proportionate?

Correct proportions are costs that operate the business day in and day out. Fixed Costs and Semi-Variable Costs remaining in the correct proportions keeps the company upright and steady based on the sales and Margin performance of the month. I will dedicate a chapter to each type of cost. For now, I will clarify the difference between them.

Margin has Fixed Costs

Fixed Costs are repeating costs that DO NOT change significantly from month to month.

Fixed Manager salaries do not change.

Fixed "Non-People Costs", such as rent, insurance, cell phone contracts, etc. do not change.

Margin has Semi-Variable Costs

Semi-Variable are costs that DO change from month to month.

Semi-Variable Costs also include manager performance bonuses.

Semi-Variable Non-People Costs, such as car repairs, office supplies, gas, etc. do change.

As Net Sales increases and decreases, Cost of Goods Sold increases and decreases.

As Cost of Goods Sold increases and decreases, the Margin increases and decreases proportionately based on company performance.

As the Margin increases and decreases, Fixed Costs remain constant... but the Semi-Variable Costs increase and decrease.

Fixed Costs only equal to Semi-Variable Costs at 100% Normal. When you achieve Financial Balance, the Net Profit will automatically follow. The Margin runs the business. Net Profit is owner's money, and is not part of the Margin.

> **Financial Balance is the condition in which different costs, Fixed Costs and Semi-Variable Costs are in correct proportions to keep the company upright and steady. At 100% Normal, Financial Balance creates the most safety for the business.**

TWO TYPES OF MARGIN: EQUALIZED AND BALANCED

Kanketa teaches "Safety First. Profit Second." You can make all the profit possible, but still lose your company to bankruptcy (as did Toys R Us, K-Mart, US Airways, Radio Shack - the list goes on). In some of these companies, the Fixed Costs were too high. In others, there wasn't sufficient Net Profit available in time to pay for the escalating out of control debts.

The Kanketa Balanced Margin keeps debt under control but...

Margin Isn't Margin Isn't Margin.

In Kanketa, there is an "Equalized Margin" and a "Balanced Margin." Both create the same profitability for the owner with the exception that a Balanced Margin is safer than an Equalized Margin.

An equalized company is a profitable company, but it is not necessarily safe from unexpected changes that happen suddenly in the marketplace.

A balanced company is both a safe, and profitable company. A Balanced Margin is the company's first line of defense and will contain the safe profit and expense levels.

EQUALIZED MARGIN AT NORMAL

An Equalized Margin is not a Balanced Margin. The Equalized Margin produces the same Net Profit result as a Balanced Margin. As long as the Net Profit is 1/3 of the Margin at Normal, your Margin is equalized, even though your Fixed and Semi-Variable Costs are not equal to each other. In both cases shown, the Net-Profit is one-third of the total Margin.

EQUALIZED MARGIN	EQUALIZED MARGIN
3 PARTS	3 PARTS
FIXED COSTS	FIXED COSTS
SEMI-VARIABLE COSTS	SEMI-VARIABLE COSTS
1/3 NET PROFIT	1/3 NET PROFIT
FIG 6.5	FIG 6.6

Example A:

Total monthly Margin is $12,000,
Monthly Fixed Costs are $5,000,
Semi-Variable Costs are $3,000,
and Net Profit of one-third of the Margin is $ 4,000.
The Margin is equalized.

Example B:

Total monthly Margin is $12,000,

Monthly Fixed Costs are $2,500,

Semi-Variable Costs are $5,500,

and the Net Profit is one-third of the Margin: $4,000.

The Margin is equalized.

A Balanced Budget at Normal sales levels exists when Fixed Costs and Semi-Variable Costs in the Margin equal each other. When this happens, Net Profit is automatically one-third of the Margin.

The three components are each exactly one-third of the total Margin at 100% Normal.

BALANCED MARGIN

3 EQUAL PARTS

1/3 FIXED COSTS

1/3 SEMI-VARIABLE COSTS

1/3 NET PROFIT

FIG 6.7

Example C:

Total monthly Margin is $12,000,
Monthly Fixed Cost budget is $4,000,
Monthly Semi-Variable Cost budget is $4,000,
Net Profit budget is one-third of the Margin $4,000.

This is when the Margin is balanced.

> **A company with an equalized Margin
> is a profitable, but not a safe company.
> A balanced company is both safe
> and profitable.**

True Story: Net Profit in an Unsafe but Equalized Budget

For 14 years Troy and Danielle ran a successful recruiting company of 27 employees in Dublin, Ohio.

The company consistently made a Net Profit every month between $8,000 and $10,000 after all expenses. Then, unexpectedly the business changed drastically for the worst when many industries sought lower labor costs in other countries. The couple had to reduce their labor force by half within 60 days to maintain the same Net Profit that they had counted on for years. Within a month after the reduction in workforce, their profit diminished to half. Following more cuts to survive, Troy and Danielle were now down to eight employees. Needless to say, the Net Profit continued to dwindle until their company went bankrupt and their building was sold at an auction.

The Net Profit remained at a consistent percent of the Margin throughout.

The percentage of Fixed Costs and Semi-Variable Costs expanded and contracted.

The company was equalized, and the Net Profit was the highest that the Margin allowed, but the budget was not balanced. Consequently, the company was not safe.

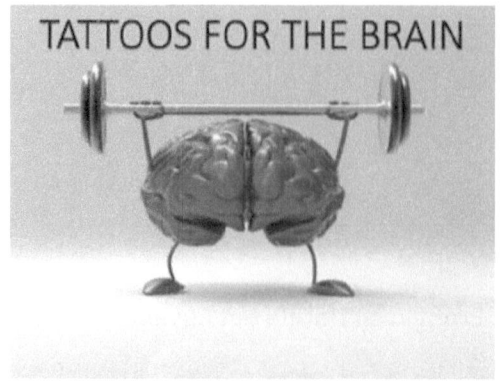

<u>THREE MARGIN TATTOOS FOR THE BRAIN</u>

Here are three takeaways for the Margin of a Kanketa Balanced Budget

#1. Margin percent of Net Sales is parallel to sales performance.

#2. Margin is the only factor that determines the growth of a business.

#3. Any expense that exceeds the monthly allowed budget becomes a debt. The Kanketa balanced Margin keeps debt under control with always enough profit in the Margin to pay for debt.

CHAPTER 7

BUDGET PART 4 OF 6
FIXED COSTS

for Budget Stability and Maintenance

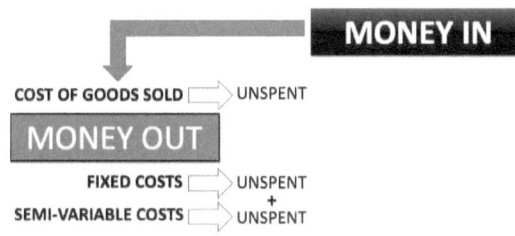

Fixed Costs Give the Company Stability

From month to month, your business has certain costs in repeating amounts that do not change significantly. These are Fixed Costs, whether you have $1 of business, or $1 million dollars of business.

Fixed Costs are the predictable, repeatable costs found in the Margin, to create and maintain company stability by keeping the doors open. If you didn't have a certain amount of your overhead costs that you could count on every month, you would be constantly doing month-to-month re-budgeting. No more than one half of your Margin overhead costs to run your company every month should be Fixed Costs.

FIXED COSTS <u>DO NOT</u> CHANGE

with sales performance

FIXED PEOPLE COSTS. FIXED "NON-PEOPLE" COSTS.

Fixed People Costs are your managers.
Fixed Non-People Costs are your operating overhead expenses.

Fixed Costs fall into two categories: Fixed People Costs (managers) and Fixed Non-People Costs (costs that aren't a person). Both are recurring costs in repeatable amounts that do not change from month to month.

FIXED PEOPLE COSTS (repeatable month to month manager's salaries)

FIXED "NON-PEOPLE" COSTS, (costs that are not a person). Repeating monthly overhead expenses necessary to maintain your business performance and profitability.

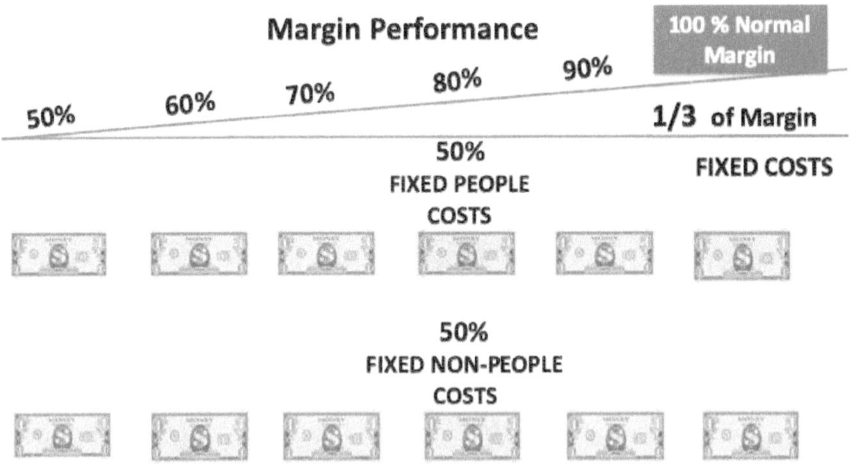

Margin Performance

100 % Normal Margin

50%   60%   70%   80%   90%

1/3 of Margin

50%
FIXED PEOPLE
COSTS

FIXED COSTS

50%
FIXED NON-PEOPLE
COSTS

FIG. 7.1

In a Kanketa Balanced Budget, Fixed People and Fixed Non-People Costs are equal to, and in balance with each other.

> Fixed People Costs in the Margin are your managers. Fixed Non-People Costs are your operating overhead expenses.

Fixed People Costs are the repeatable salaries of your managers who must show up for work, whether you sell $1 or $1 million. Their work is spread over all jobs.

Manager Salaries

Many small businesses pay salaries according to market demand; not what they can afford. Typically, this is because many businesses are not structured to make money. Redundancy and inefficiency are built into their business system.

In the 1940s, following World War II, when millions of Americans returned to work, there were severe job shortages. The U.S. way of life redesigned itself. Family-run businesses were organized and grew from loving parents who wanted to provide for their children. They built their companies with the sole purpose of creating secure jobs, but not necessarily with the vision of creating significant financial futures. Out of this survival motivation grew our American college-taught organization chart which is used today. I prefer to call this the "Importance Chart."

If you inherited a business and nearly all of your business knowledge came from hard-working parents; or you started a business and learned it by osmosis; or you went to a business college and learned it in a business theory class; or perhaps you had a mentor who had a successful business career back when, you have probably been taught the Importance Chart along the way.

The Importance Chart is a traditional hierarchical business model borrowed from large companies by small companies, purely from the lack of any other useful business model. In my opinion this corporate flow chart does not work, nor does it have a place in today's small business world. By its very design, it promotes separation and creates walls between people who should be in constant collaboration. It is a model of who's more important, who's making more money and who can't talk to whom.

THE IMPORTANCE CHART

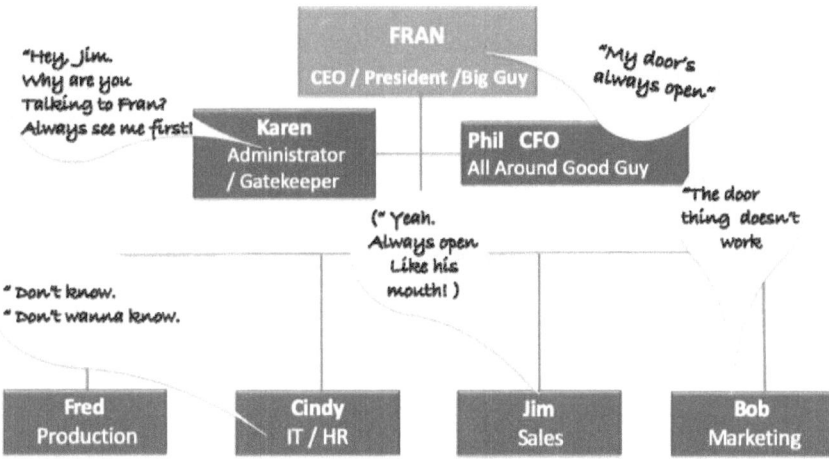

Ever since I can remember, this business model has always bothered me. In the 1960s, the guy at the end of the hall with the big window was the important guy. He had the most pictures on his wall, and a new grey carpet. The important guy made the most money.

Back then, your importance was visible to the company based on the location of your office, the size and type of pictures on your wall, and the color of the furniture in your room. Grey carpet and couches and leather chairs with brass studded arm rests were for the most important people, followed by navy and Naugahyde. People's earnings were reflected by the color of their rooms.

Meaningless titles were on every business card. Few people in the company had true empowerment. Isn't It amazing how banks and insurance companies can have so many Vice Presidents who can't make decisions?

Clearly, the leadership methods were very different back then. If you ever have a chance to watch the TV series "Madmen", you'll know what I mean. The series premiered on July 19, 2007 on cable network AMC. The show was extremely well produced. The producers didn't miss a detail. If you want to understand how companies were managed in the 1960s, watch this series.

Business was operated and managed under the importance system. It was nothing but a political fishbowl. Prevailing attitudes of employees were "I don't dare to contribute. I don't care to contribute. I'd better just shut my mouth, do my job and collect my paycheck. I don't want to get fired for my opinions".

Ironically, the big guy at the end of the hall would periodically stick his head out of the door and yell, "My door is always open." All the while, the employees were saying to themselves under their breath ... "yeah, and you need to get that door hinge fixed".

 **FLAT ORGANIZATIONS**
not

FLAT JOB DESCRIPTIONS!

No Empowerment.   Political.   Just do your job.

"Is my business set up to make a profit?"

There are millions of businesses that make a healthy profit without the Kanketa method. You don't need Kanketa to be successful. That said, I'd like to take a page or two to explain the question: Is my business set up to make a profit? Am I in complete control of the profit that I expect, or does Net Profit just show up?"

Flat Organization

Kanketa promotes the idea of a "flat organization" as a specific way to look at and operate a business so that it always maintains a healthy balance of accountability and empowerment between everyone who works in it. In Kanketa, every employee contributes and is compensated on equal terms (not necessarily in equal amounts).

Why should you bother with this, if it's going to create more work for you? Do you really want more accountability? Are you looking to wrap yourself around the discomfort of change? Why not just run the business the way you've always done it and continue to make money? In fact, why have employees at all? Just make it YOU and avoid the hassle. Many solopreneurs brag about how much money they make without having to deal with the headaches of employees. Please hear me out. There is significant long-term reward waiting for you for enduring the difficult process of building a staff of loyal, key employees.

True Story: Build Workrooms, Not Walls

Steve W. of Bloomington, Illinois. had three full time managers plus himself in his retail shop. The managers were required to show up whether there was $1 or $1 million dollars of business.

When Steve bought the company three years before, he inherited the problems of existing positions. One of the managers was his brother-in-law. The other two were in the family of the friend from whom he bought the company.

There were no clear positions or job descriptions. Since nothing was written, every day was a fight over who was doing what, when and why. Misunderstandings ran high over who was contributing more. Much time was wasted daily over arguments of the smallest responsibilities. Production errors escalated by default. Eventually, the managers quit and started their own competitive companies. Over the next ten years, the owners of each of their own companies made the equivalent of what they would have made as a salary working for Steve, without a decade of hassle and ill-feelings.

The difference between a high-performing, high-profit company and any company that is not growing, just going, is clarity of responsibilities set in place, in writing, on day one. In a balanced company, no management position is, or should be, worth more or less than any other. In Kanketa, every manager receives the same Fixed base salary for fundamental responsibilities... to keep the company safe. Each manager is individually empowered to earn more than their fixed base salary based on company performance.

THE KANKETA HOUSE OF VALUE

The KANKETA ideogram tells many stories.

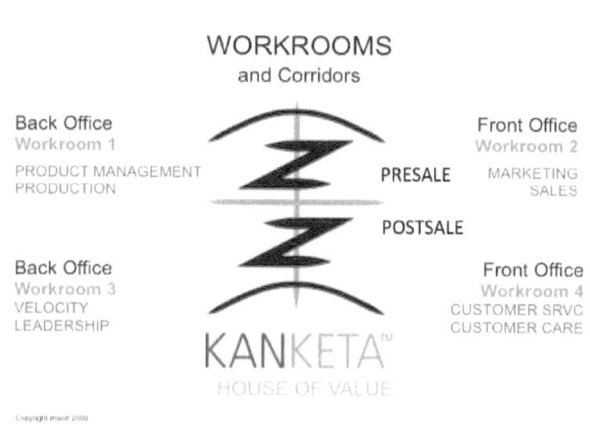

FIG 7.2

This ideogram is a business plan, a financial plan, an organizational plan, a physical store, a physical office and a plant layout, a leadership model and many other constructs. For our purposes, we will see this symbol as a business structure and a design for a "House of Value," with virtual rooms and walls, doors and corridors.

"How many managers do I need?"

THE ANSWER: Ultimately, enough managers to efficiently carry out the eight basic functions of every business on the globe, for starters. Four managers will be needed in a company of 30 employees or less, one for each Workroom.

The Kanketa House of Value is divided into four equal and inseparable parcels "Workrooms", which are connecting rooms of equal size. The Workrooms each carry out one of the four functional business purposes: make something, sell something, deliver something and service someone.

Over the years I have observed successful Kanketa-based small companies with no more than four managers, efficiently, effectively and consistently producing up to $5 million a year in Gross Sales.

FIG 7.3

Each Workroom is divided into two "corridors". Each Workroom is managed by a Workroom Manager. Each Workroom Manager oversees and carries out two related job descriptions for delivering a specific result. There is one overarching, primary, measurable performance result expected from each corridor.

Each manager is responsible for the two corridors in their Workroom.

The lower corridor in each Workroom relies on its upper big sister corridor to produce a result, before its functions can be can fully and effectively carried out.

In the Kanketa model...

- a business will need marketing before sales,
- product management before production,
- velocity (delivery) before self-directed leadership,
- customer service before customer care.

Top corridor first. Bottom corridor second.

A Business Leader is needed at the center of the house to keep all the corridors in motion, to carry out the vision and mission of the owner, and to report to the owner.

BACK OFFICE. FRONT OFFICE.

The back office, upper and lower Workrooms on the left side of the House, is comprised of the MAKE and DELIVER responsibilities. In the upper and lower Workrooms in the front office, there are the SELL and SERVICE responsibilities. The front office deals with the marketplace and shakes hands with the public. The back-office people serve and treat the front office people as their internal customers.

House Rules

Any manager may participate in any Workroom where they are needed, when they are needed. However, there is always one Workroom Manager who is the ultimate authority, with the overriding responsibility for his/her Workroom. Each Workroom is equal to and inseparable from the others.

In the Kanketa House of Value, no Workroom is of greater or lesser importance, nor are the people in it.

INDIRECT EMPLOYEES

Indirect employees must show up for work whether there is one job, or a hundred jobs, whether you sell $1 or $1 million dollars. An indirect employee may be full time or part time. Your managers are your "indirect" employees. They must show up come rain or come shine, whether you have no work or a lot of work. Their work effort is spread out over the entire company. They do parts of all the jobs needed to run the company. They are hired to do whatever is needed, and whatever it takes.

Headcount

There is a practice among large companies to balance their budgets by managing and measuring overall productivity and controlling profit by headcount. Headcount says that the total sales of the company divided by the number of people in the company equals the average dollar amount that each person is contributing.

Headcount numbers are measured against national averages across each industry to determine the number of people that the company should keep employed. Companies hire and fire on this basis. This practice allows some accountant to make financial decisions without considering who is being hired and fired and why. Jack Welch of GE automatically fired the 10 percent lowest performers without looking sideways, no questions asked.

My perspective only: Considering that it costs five times to more define, identify, locate, interview, qualify, verify, propose to, hire, onboard and train a new employee, than it does to retrain and re-motivate an existing one, companies of 30 or less should focus on retraining, reassigning and repurposing if possible. Hint: start by having the employees take the Gallup Strengthsfinder test found online. This might open some eyes.

Repositioning Talent

Perhaps, rather than replacing an underperforming employee in one area of the business, they can be trained in another area of the company. For example, if they are underperforming in production, perhaps they might be successful in marketing the business or in sales. The owner of a Kanketa-managed business will do everything possible to take the high road, rather than firing a person because of some headcount-to-profit ratio.

Let the large companies crumble under their own weight. Let their accountants play by worn and dated rules. Balancing a company by headcount might make sense to some bean counters, but to me, headcount has no place in the Kanketa House of Value for today's high performing small business.

CORRIDOR TEAMS

In Kanketa, the Corridor teams are uniquely defined and rewarded for performance by the business owner. Some companies design and reward their teams vertically, pairing a team member from an upper Workroom with a team from a lower Workroom (example of pairing: Product Manager from the MAKE Workroom collaborates with the Velocity Manager from the DELIVER Workroom). Others choose a horizontal team approach, setting up and rewarding front office and back office managers for individual as well as team performance.

FIG 7.4

In a collaborative team effort, Marketing complements Sales. Marketing in the upper SELL Workroom can also work well with Customer Service.

Sales in the upper SELL Workroom (Pre-sale) can also work well with Customer Care (Post Sale). In a team, Product Management complements Production. Product Management in the upper MAKE Workroom (Pre-Sale) can also work well with Velocity (DELIVERY) in the lower Workroom (Post-Sale).

While team missions differ from business to business, in all cases, there are specific job functions that complement each other.

Manager Pay Scales

Standing back, this model creates one big question about employee compensation. If the Workrooms and Corridors are equal and inseparable, if no one is more or less important than the other, if every Corridor is ultimately responsible to deliver a single result, if everyone is accountable and empowered and if the company is truly a balanced, flat organization – then what about salaries? Is anyone paid more or less than the others?

Each of the four Workroom Managers in the Kanketa House of Value is initially responsible for carrying out two job descriptions. One half of a Workroom Manager's job or 10 hours a week is the maximum time budgeted to maintain the performance of one Corridor in a Workroom. Maintaining the performance of two Corridors should take one manager less than 20 hours a week. Once a company hovers around 30 employees, the Corridor responsibilities begin to expand and require their own full-time Corridor Managers.

Begin by Paying Managers for Two Workrooms

Kanketa expects at least 75% of every week to result in specific, measurable financial increases for the company by each manager. In Kanketa, a Workroom Manager will spend four hours a week, managing a Corridor in meetings, and in non-value-added time, with 16 hours of on-the-job billable time to its internal and external customers.

> *"I am both an owner and a manager in my business.*
> *How much should I pay myself?"*

This depends upon what Corridors you cover, and why and how you pay yourself.

The answer is: pay yourself a salary separately as a Workroom Manager who works in the company on a daily basis. Pay yourself from the Net Profit as the owner. More to come on this.

Corridors of Responsibility

What Corridors in your House of Value are you personally covering every day when you work in your business? What are you most passionate about when you work in your business?

Are you most passionate about ...

Product Management? Researching and creating new products? Finding and managing suppliers?

Production? Doing the work hands on? Ensuring that each product is error free?

Velocity? Scheduling and delivery of products and services?

Human Resources? Ensuring that employees are happy and productive?

Marketing? Finding and creating new opportunities from new, first time prospects?

Sales? Proposing and closing jobs and converting prospects into paying contracts?

Customer Service? Making sure that each new customer is satisfied with every transaction during their experience?

Customer Care? Creating reasons to have customers keep coming back?

Don't pay more to yourself for any of these positions than you pay to other managers. You'll create imbalance if you do. When you eventually decide to replace yourself, you will be using your salary to pay a Workroom Manager as your replacement.

I will cover this topic later in the Net Profit chapter.

Manager Salaries

Once again, Fixed People Costs are the (pre-tax) gross salaries that must be paid to any indirect employees whether you have $1 of business, or $1 million dollars of business. The People Costs in your Margin are salaries for your managers.

Now, you are probably asking yourself, "Aren't my managers' salaries a Fixed Cost? They are paid the same salary from month to month." The answer is yes, and maybe.

Yes, your Fixed People Costs are the salaries in the Margin that do not change from month to month. However, in Kanketa, not everything that is paid to your managers is a Fixed salary. Kanketa does not support, promote nor encourage the idea of totally Fixed salaries. Instead, based on manager responsibilities, Kanketa divides a manager's compensation equally into 50% Fixed salary and 50% as compensation for team performance. In Kanketa, the Fixed manager salaries (paid one time monthly by the 10th day) are for maintaining company performance and to keep the Gross Sales, Margin and Net Profit of the company from slipping.

Fixed People Costs are in place to ensure that the company doesn't lose money while it continues to grow. In Kanketa, the company owner approves a specific list of maintenance work, everything that it takes to prevent each position, each Workroom and the total company performance from declining in productivity and profitability.

Fixed salaries pay for loss prevention activities. All other compensation to managers is pay for performance for the growth of the company.

> **Pay managers 50% of their total compensation for maintaining their Workroom performance, and additional compensation for increasing company performance and profitability.**

True Story: Out of Balance Fixed Costs Can Really Fix You... For Good!

Jason L, of Lansing, Michigan inherited his father's bicycle shop of 18 years. In his effort to create an efficient hands-off business, Jason negotiated as many costs as possible to be Fixed. Jason believed that if all of his costs were the same from month to month, his bookkeeping would be a breeze and he'd have less accounting work to do. The salaries of his 5 employees were the same every month. His operating costs were the same. He held to a strict auto allowance that didn't change, a rigid office expense budget with a Fixed budget for trash pickup, office supplies and a Fixed monthly retainer for his accountant.

Every annual bill was divided by 12 and he sent the payments monthly. This was fine at first. Sales were stable and steady from month to month and Jas made a nice profit. Later as the months went by, the bicycle industry started to change. The market's appetite for the younger bikes in Jason's inventory went to lighter weight exercise bikes for older people. Added to this the increased price of steel increased the cost of new inventories with a whole new line of tools to repair them. Sales gradually declined to an average of 60% of Normal levels and Jason had to lay off his technicians. Since everyone was so acclimated to a steady paycheck, there was no flexibility to negotiate wages. In the following year Jason was down to 2 technicians and had to move to a small location half the size. The Net Profit declined.

Jason's company was too anchored with Fixed Costs. By not balancing his business, he was unable to move with the changing market. This inflexibility is the same problem that unions create.

NOTE: All case studies used in this book are based on actual situations. The names and business types in the examples have been slightly altered to protect the business owners.

FIXED NON-PEOPLE COSTS

Non-People Costs are all recurring overhead operating expenses of the business that are not People Costs. Rent is a Fixed Non-People Cost that does not change. An insurance payment is a Fixed Non-People Cost that does not change. Cellphone contracts are Fixed Non-People Costs that do not change. Leases are Fixed Non-People Costs that do not change. Whether sales are way up, or way down, these are Fixed Costs that are constant and unchanging from month to month.

Main Non-People Fixed Cost Categories:

1. Advertising
2. Insurances (other than health)
3. Interest
4. Monthly Office Service Contracts
5. Equipment and Vehicle Leases
6. Office Lease or Rent
7. Fixed Loan Payments
8. Depreciation
9. Miscellaneous – All Other

Sub-categories of Expenses

Within each of these main cost categories are subcategories of expense items. For example, in the Monthly Office Service Contracts, there are Fixed Costs such as recurring cell phone contracts, and monthly waste management contracts. In Equipment and Vehicle Leases there are car leases, and computer leases. In the Office Service contracts category, you will find Fixed contracts for outside services such as monthly cleaning and computer maintenance contracts, and so on.

If you are going to list anything alphabetically, make the sub-categories alphabetical.

"How much should I pay for rent?"

Out-Of-Home Office Rent

While some would argue that rent depends upon the type of business you are in, I will present a more static approach. I will confine the discussion of rent to workspace for managers.

In a company of 30 employees or less, you will need a maximum of 4 managers and one Business Leader to operate your company up to your 100% Normal Margin level (Net Sales minus Cost of Goods Sold). These people are brought into the company over time. With over 30 employees, the Workrooms will begin to require more management and more staff.

Beyond the basic office space for these managers, the remaining (extended) rent costs are industry specific. Warehouse space, retail space, technology and other production space follow their own guidelines when constructing budgets. We will use "extended workspace" as a general label and give extended workspace its own account code. In this case you will have two rent payments: one that will always remain constant (for managers) and one that might change based on company growth.

Returning to the Discussion of Office Space...

an 80 square foot office area (8' X 10' or 9' X 9'), organized properly, should accommodate one efficient, productive Workroom Manager.

The Math:

Divide your average monthly rent ($200 country average) by usable necessary square footage (80 Sq. Ft) to determine usable office space per square foot. If minimum monthly rent for one manager is $200 and the manager's office has 80 square feet of usable space, you're paying $2.50 per square foot. The same area should be ample for a Business Leader. In other words, for an office-only, 4-manager rent allocation for 30 employees, the rent budget would be $1,000 in the Kanketa Balanced Budget. We will call everything else industry-specific Production Workspace. The difference between budgets is determined by where you live. The $2.50 square foot cost in Arkansas for 80 square feet will cost more in New York. This should be taken into consideration when you are budgeting your workspace.

Examples of Sub-Contracts within the main heading of

RECURRING MONTHLY CONTRACTS

- Cleaning - Janitorial Services
- Dues and Subscriptions
- Internet Service
- Phone - Landline
- Phone - cell
- Security
- Software Licenses
- Technology Service Contracts
- Waste Removal

One Time Annual Fees

You probably have some annual contracts for something. Maybe it's an annual software license or an advertising contract. One time Fixed annual charges should be divided by twelve to get a monthly Fixed Cost average. You will want to do this for a couple of reasons:

1. **30-Day Business Expenses.**

Everything breaks down to a monthly cost. This is helpful because, after a year or certain period of time when a Fixed contract comes up for renewal, you will have accumulated enough money each month in your checking account to pay for it. One twelfth (1/12) of the payment is the average monthly amount that you will not be spending in your Fixed Cost budget that should accumulate toward the annual fee.

2. **Fixed Costs Might Change Slightly**

I said that Fixed salaries are People Costs that do not change from month to month. Realistically, some salaries might not remain exactly the same to the penny for the year. You might have a good reason to increase a person's Fixed salary during the year. Certain Fixed Non-People Costs could also change during the year. You might get a notice for a rent increase. A cellphone might be added to your contract. Insurance rates can go up.

A Fixed maintenance contract that costs $150 a month year around might have a month here and there that it increases to $165 because of an unforeseen circumstance.

There are a host of different reasons for Fixed Cost increases.

The budget categories themselves can be individually adjusted to manage small increases here and there. The goal is to not allow the total of the main Fixed Non-People expense categories to get out of balance with the total Fixed People salaries. For the sake of practicality, let's say that all Fixed Costs generally do not fluctuate by more than 5% in any month from the previous month.

> **Fixed Costs generally do not fluctuate from month to month by more than 5%.**

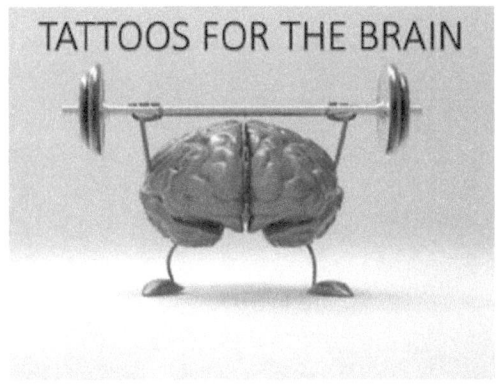

TATTOOS FOR THE BRAIN

THREE FIXED COST TATTOOS FOR THE BRAIN

Here are three takeaways for the Fixed Costs of a Kanketa Balanced Budget

#1. In a Kanketa Balanced Budget, Fixed People Costs and Fixed Non-People Costs are equal to each other.

#2. The Kanketa system compensates Managers with a Fixed salary for maintaining the performance of their departments. Managers are paid additional performance pay for increasing the performance of their departments and the company as a whole.

#3. Fixed Costs do not fluctuate from month to month by more than 5%.

CHAPTER 8

BUDGET PART 5 OF 6
SEMI-VARIABLE COSTS

for Budget Flexibility and Growth

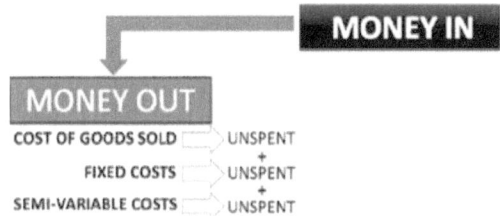

All along I have been talking about costs that do not change significantly from month to month. Yet, from month to month, your business also has overhead costs that <u>DO</u> change.

Semi-Variable Costs are company expense types that you will always have, but they will change slightly every month, up and down, with the sales performance of the business.

SEMI-VARIABLE COSTS DO CHANGE FROM MONTH TO MONTH

SEMI-VARIABLE PEOPLE COSTS (managers' pay that changes with business performance)

SEMI-VARIABLE NON-PEOPLE COSTS - costs that are not a person (changing monthly overhead expenses necessary to grow your business and increase your profitability)

UTILITIES?

OFFICE SUPPLIES?

AUTO MAINTENANCE?

POSTAGE? ETC.

SEMI-VARIABLE COSTS <u>DO</u> CHANGE

slightly with sales performance

When sales are higher than 100% Normal, you will put more gas in your car to service existing customers. When your sales are lower than 100% Normal, you will use less gas to service those customers. When your sales are higher than 100% Normal, you will use more postage, more office supplies, more electricity. When your sales are lower than 100% Normal, you will use less postage, fewer office supplies, and less electricity.

You will always have these types of Semi-Variable operating costs, but they will move up and down slightly as the sales of your company increases and decreases. These costs are called Semi-Variable because they are always there, but they breathe with the performance of your business.

SEMI-VARIABLE COSTS ARE ONLY FOUND IN THE MARGIN

Main Semi-Variable Cost Categories (only in the Margin):

1. Manager Performance Pay
2. Employee Benefits
3. Office Supplies
4. Professional Fees
5. General Repairs and Maintenance (not vehicles)
6. Taxes, and Licenses (no state sales tax)
7. Vehicle Repairs and Maintenance
8. Travel (cost of vehicle operation: fuel, oil, parking etc.)
9. Customer Meals and Entertainment
10. Utilities
11. Miscellaneous – all other

The Goal of a Balanced Budget.

The goal is to make Fixed People Costs equal to Semi-Variable People Costs and Fixed Non-People Costs equal to Semi-Variable Non-People Costs at 100% Normal performance.

Budget 10 hours a week per manager to maintain each of their two Corridors and 10 hours a week per manager to grow each Corridor. Expect 75% total result-oriented billable time each week from every manager.

> **Fixed Costs pay for maintaining company stability and getting it safe. Semi-Variable Costs pay for keeping the company safe and creating growth.**

MANAGER PERFORMANCE COMPENSATION
(For Creating Company Safety)

"Am I paying (my people) too much? Not enough?"
"How much should I pay my people?"

Semi-Variable People Costs: Performance Compensation for Company Safety

The question isn't "How much should I pay my people?" A better question to ask is "How much am I willing to pay my people to help me get my business safe and to keep my business safe?" These are two separate questions.

Getting to a safe position and keeping a safe position are accomplished by ensuring that the company has increased opportunities to win by increasing Gross Sales and Margin while reducing costs. Kanketa encourages that employee salaries are balanced, with one-half paid for maintenance to get the company to a safe and stable position, and one-half performance to keep the company in a safe position and in a growth mode.

By balancing a manager's maintenance responsibilities with a list of growth activities, including everything it takes to grow the profitability of the employee's position and the Workroom, you will create an overall consistent company performance.

Need some free ideas? Call me. My number is in the back of the book.

PEOPLE COSTS: MANAGER PERFORMANCE PAY

Pay Managers One-Half of Their Compensation to Maintain the Business (Safety)

"If the company is safe, our jobs are safe".

In Kanketa, one-half of a Workroom Manager's job ... or 10 hours a week per Corridor is budgeted to ensure that the Corridor and the company doesn't slide backward and lose money. This protection takes a specific list of manager tasks that must be carried out.

... and One Half to Grow the Business

"If the company makes money, we all make money".

The other half of a Workroom Manager's job, or 10 hours a week for each corridor should be dedicated to grow the company and increase Margin and profit. This is a specific list of manager tasks that are carried out.

IF SALES ARE AT 100% NORMAL, EACH MANAGER EARNS 100% OF THEIR MONTHLY WAGES,

which is 4.17% of NORMAL Monthly Margin, as a FIXED salary,

and 4.17% of NORMAL Monthly Margin, as a PERFORMANCE BONUS.

In other words, at Normal the managers are paid equally for maintaining and for bringing the company to safety.

IF SALES ARE AT LESS THAN 100% NORMAL, EACH MANAGER EARNS 4.17% of NORMAL Monthly Margin as a FIXED salary that doesn't change from month to month and 4.17% of the MARGIN percent of the previous month's company performance as a PERFORMANCE BONUS.

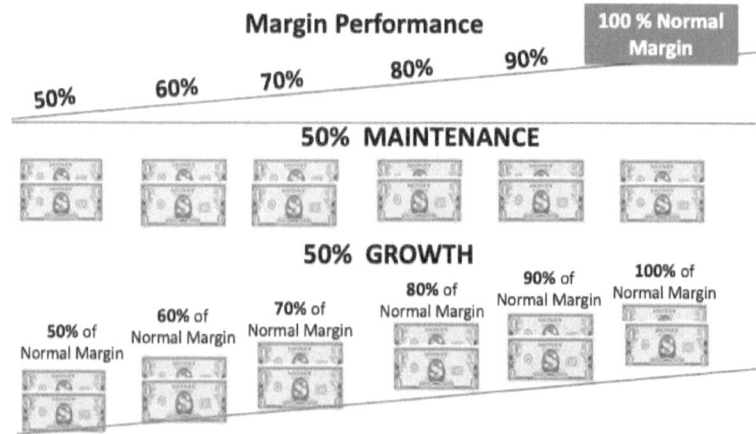

FIG. 8.1

Individual and Team Performance Pay

"If others do not perform, are they limiting my potential?".

Some global companies balance Workrooms further by balancing manager growth compensation between Semi-Variable team contribution and Semi-Variable individual performance. In this way, if the team isn't performing, the individual isn't held back from overachieving. Conversely, if the individual is underperforming, the team isn't penalized.

In the previous example, the performance compensation is split evenly between all managers. But, what happens when one manager is responsible for 60% of all company growth? In this case, the managers are each rewarded accordingly from the total available Semi-Variable People performance bonus pool according to their own individual contribution. If an over-achieving manager is responsible for 60% of the growth for the month, the manager deserves 60% of the month's total performance pay bucket at each sales level of the company.

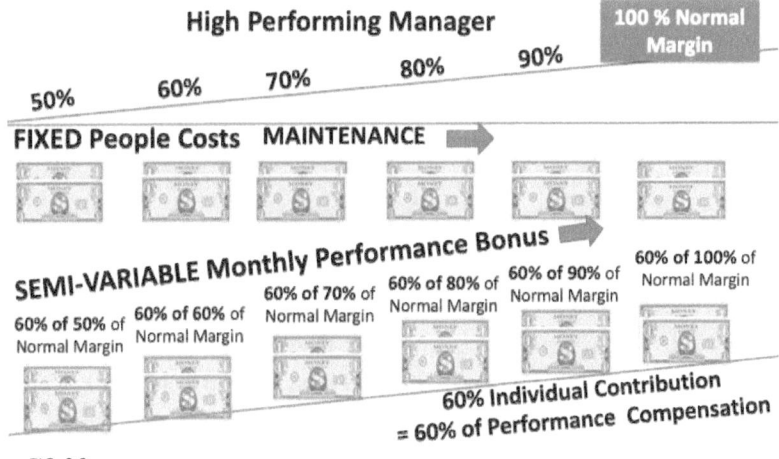

FIG. 8.2

This is proven to be an effective structure, since a poorly performing team may not hold back a high-performing individual, and a low-performing individual may not put drag on a high-performing team.

GIVING RAISES

"When can I give my employees a raise? How Much?"

Give raises once a year to everyone on the management team based on the prior year's performance. In Kanketa, everyone gets a raise at the same time with the new budget because raises are based on Margins, not emotions.

In the previous chapter on Fixed Costs, I established that 50% of your people compensation at Normal should be Fixed. In Kanketa, any more than this throws the compensation budget out of balance and the company's safety out the window. The company is overpaying for less value than it is receiving.

Kanketa teaches that managers should have performance bonuses when they do a good job. Consequently, their bonus compensation would logically be different from month to month. Semi-Variable "People" compensation is the (pre-tax) gross pay to your managers for their ability to grow the company. Semi-Variable pay is performance pay.

How much of a raise?

In Kanketa, the purpose of Semi-Variable compensation to managers is to reward them for increased company performance. Before you give a raise, be sure your FIXED salary levels are 8.33% of Margin at Normal (.0833 X Margin) for every active manager that you have hired for a Workroom – (from 1 to 4 managers including you as the owner). The goal is to cover all Workrooms first with the available people who you trust to manage the company.

Once you have put your trustworthy employees in place and all Workrooms are assigned, put Semi-Variable Performance Compensation in place. Your managers are now being paid equally to maintain and paid individually for performance to grow their Workrooms.

At a glance...

Margin at 100% Normal X 4.17% is the monthly Fixed salary paid to each manager to maintain his/her Workroom. Fixed salaries are paid by the 10th of the month.

Performance Margin X 4.17% is the manager's monthly Semi-Variable Performance Compensation to grow their Workroom. This is based on previous month's performance and is paid on or before the 25th.

MANAGER PERFORMANCE COMPENSATION SCHEDULE

PERFORMANCE COMPENSATION – PAY 4.17% OF PERFORMANCE MARGIN

In Kanketa, once a month, by the 25th, each manager receives the second half of his/her pay for improving the profitability of their department. Performance compensation is based on the company's previous month's Margin.

1. The previous month's Margin is **100%** of Margin at 100% Normal.
   Example: At a Margin of **$95,000** at Normal, the manager's performance compensation by the 25th of the following month will be $95,000 X **100%** Normal Margin X .0417 manager performance pay (in this case: **$3,962**).

2. The previous month's Margin is **90%-99%** of the above 100% Normal Margin.
   Example: At a Margin that falls between $85,500 and $94,999, the manager's performance compensation on the 25th of the following month will be $95,000 X **90%** of Normal Margin X .0417 (in this case: **$3,565**).

3. The previous month's Margin is **80%-89%** of the above 100% Normal Margin.
   Example: At a Margin that falls between $76,000 and $85,499, the manager's performance compensation by the 25th of the following month will be $95,000 X **80%** of Normal Margin X .0417 (in this case: **$3,169**).

4. The previous month's Margin is **70%-79%** of the above 100% Normal Margin.
   Example: At a Margin that falls between $66,500 and $75,999, the manager's performance compensation on the 25th of the following month will be $95,000 X **70%** of Normal Margin X .0417 (in this case: **$2,773**).

5. The previous month's Margin is **60%-69%** of the above 100% Normal Margin.
   Example: At a Margin that falls between $57,000 and $66,499, the manager's performance compensation on the 25th of the following month will be $95,000 X **60%** of Normal Margin X .0417 (in this case: **$2,377**).

6. The previous month's Margin is **50%-59%** of the above 100% Normal Margin.
   Example: At a Margin that falls between $47,500 - $56,999, the manager's performance compensation on the 25th of the following month will be $95,000 X **50%** of Normal Margin X .0417 (in this case: **$1,981**).

SEMI-VARIABLE NON-PEOPLE OVERHEAD
(TO SUPPORT COMPANY SAFETY)

The purpose of Semi-Variable budgeting is to ensure that you do not spend more than you can afford. In Kanketa, the Semi-Variable Non-People expenses are the routine, familiar monthly repeating operational costs (although they might not be as predictable or repeatable as your Fixed Costs). These costs will change slightly up or down with sales performance.

Semi-Variable Non-People Costs in the Margin are all overhead costs that support growth as the sales performance of the business increases. Semi-Variable Non-People Costs can produce and control cost savings. Semi-Variable Non-People Costs are the biggest constituents for a Balanced Budget.

Transparency with Employees

The People budgets are equal for all Workrooms. The Non-People budgets are equal throughout the company.

I believe in transparency with employees whenever possible. Employees talk and eventually they will all hear the story. You might as well accurately present your side up front so that they all hear it in the way that you intend it to be heard.

If you are an employer who chooses to be private with your employees when discussing compensation, this information will give you a tool for giving individual raises privately as you see individual progress and effort. Because your Cost of Goods budget proportionately follows your sales performance percentage of 100% Normal, your monthly Margin should also reflect the sales performance percentage. If it doesn't, your Cost of Goods Sold might not be well managed. Keep in mind that while your Margin is in proportion to sales, your Fixed Non-People Costs in your Margin always remain consistent, while your Semi-Variable Non-People Costs are changing based on the company performance of the previous month.

The significant benefit of Semi-Variable Cost management is that you always stay within your budget, based on the previous month's performance. By staying within your Semi-Variable budget, you will never spend money you don't have.

Job Safety

Many large global companies begin layoffs at approximately 70% of Normal Gross Sales performance. The Kanketa budget is designed so that at any performance level above 50% of Normal, which is all costs including manager compensation, are always paid. In other words, at 50% of Normal performance, a manager will still have a job if the company's sales suddenly and unexpectedly dropped to half.

As long as the company sells more than 50% of its Normal Monthly Margin, the company can afford up to 4 managers at 75% of their Normal compensation without layoffs. For up to three consecutive months.

Most Japanese companies, using similar Kanketa models, like Toyota, Suzuki, Kawasaki, etc. kept all of their employees in place following the tsunami which devastated Japan in 2011.

Company Safety

Semi-Variable Costs apply to Non-People expenses as well. The only time that Fixed Costs and Semi-Variable Costs are equal to each other is in the budget at 100% Normal. All the rest of the time, while Fixed People and Fixed Non-People Costs do not change, the Semi-Variable People and Non-People Costs are budgeted to change at each sales performance level.

THE KANKETA GOLDEN RULE:

Last Month's Performance (Total NET SALES) Determines This Month's Budget.

Sales will rise and fall according to industry seasonality and unexpected circumstances. In Kanketa, the Semi-Variable People and Non-People Costs increase and decrease slightly from one month to the next with sales performance. We have seen how the managers are paid accordingly in the following month from the Semi-Variable percentage as overall sales performance increases or decreases in one month.

If your business performs at 70% of Normal in a month, then your business can only afford to pay 70% of your budgeted Semi-Variable People costs at Normal, paid in the following month. Fixed Costs remain the same.

If the overall business increases in a month by 10% above Normal performance, then your business can afford 110% of your budgeted Semi-Variable People costs at Normal, paid in the following month. This Semi-Variable process also applies to Non-People overhead in the same manner.

Here's another example.

If your Net Sales is 60% of Normal in a month, then you should only allow 60% of the Normal budget for your overhead for the following month. In this case your Non-People budget in the following month would be 60% for gas for the car, 60% for office supplies, 60% for utilities, etc. If your Net Sales is 120% of Normal in a month, then you may allow 120% of your Normal budget for your overhead for the following month.

In this case your Non-People budget in the following month would be 120% for gas for the car, 120% for office supplies, 120% for utilities, etc.

HOW FIXED AND SEMI-VARIABLE COSTS FIT TOGETHER AT "NORMAL"

EXAMPLE: WHEN COMPARING A NORMAL SALES MONTH, BEGIN WITH...

(Budget Set Up in January from Last Year's 12 Month Monthly Average)

ANNUAL SALES TARGET at Normal $ **720,000**

MONTHLY SALES Target at Normal $ **60,000**
MONTHLY COST OF QUALITY (budgeted at Normal) $ 1,000
MONTHLY COST OF GOODS SOLD (budgeted at Normal) $ 14,000

MONTHLY MARGIN at Normal $ 45,000

1/3 FIXED (at Normal) $ 15,000

    50% of FIXED = PEOPLE (All Managers) $ 7,500
    Each Manager is paid ½ FIXED SALARY
    (4.17% of NORMAL MARGIN) $ 1,875

    50% of FIXED = NON-PEOPLE $ 7,500
    For Monthly Operating Overhead Expenses that stay the same
    Advertising, Rent, Insurance, etc.

1/3 SEMI-VARIABLE (at Normal) $ 15,000

    50% of SEMI-VARIABLE = PEOPLE (All Managers) $ 7,500
    Each Manager is paid ½ SEMI-VARIABLE PERFORMANCE PAY
    (4.17% of NORMAL MARGIN) $ 1,875

    50% of SEMI-VARIABLE = NON-PEOPLE $ 7,500
    For Monthly Operating Overhead Expenses that change

1/3 NET PROFIT
$45,000 MARGIN minus $15,000 FIXED
minus $15,000 Semi-Variable = $ 15,000

> **Your current monthly budget is determined by last month's Net Sales performance as it increases or decreases from 100% Normal performance.**

WHAT HAPPENS WHEN YOU SELL
MORE OR LESS THAN 100% NORMAL IN A MONTH?

(Example)

NORMAL MONTH's NET SALES	$ 60,000
MONTHLY COST OF QUALITY (budgeted at Normal)	$ 1,000
MONTHLY COST OF GOODS SOLD (budgeted at Normal)	$ 14,000
NORMAL MONTHLY MARGIN	**$ 45,000**

Sales Performance in May: 82% of NORMAL NET SALES PERFORMANCE (above)

LAST MONTH's ACTUAL SALES (82% of $60,000 above)	**$ 49,200**
MONTHLY COST OF QUALITY (82% of $1000 above)	$ 820
MONTHLY COST OF GOODS SOLD (82% of $14,000 above)	$ 11,480
82% of NORMAL MONTHLY MARGIN at Sales Performance	**$ 36,900**

1/3 of Normal Margin ($45,000) = ALL FIXED COSTS (do not change)

$ 15,000

50% of 1/3 Fixed = FIXED PEOPLE (All Managers)	**$ 7,500**
Each Manager is paid FIXED SALARY	
(4.17% of NORMAL MARGIN)	$ 1,875
50% FIXED NON-PEOPLE	**$ 7,500**

For Monthly Operating Overhead Expenses
Advertising
Rent
Insurance, etc.

1/3 of Normal Margin ($45,000) = SEMI-VARIABLE COSTS (do change)
82% of $15,000 = SEMI-VARIABLE

$ 12,300

50% SEMI-VARIABLE PEOPLE (Available for all managers)	**$ 6,150**
50% SEMI-VARIABLE NON-PEOPLE	**$ 6,150**

For Monthly Operating Overhead Expenses that change

1/3 NET PROFIT at 82%

MARGIN ($36,900) minus FIXED ($15,000) minus Semi-Variable ($12,300)

$ 9,600

By calculating your MONTHLY BUDGET

using your performance percentage against NORMAL,

you will always know month-to-month

how much you can afford to spend

and keep your company safe.

OVERSPENT AND UNSPENT:
WHEN COSTS DON'T FIT THE BUDGET

It will be rare that Fixed Costs exactly equal Semi-Variable Costs. One will almost always exceed the other. This is handled by simply adding an additional "Unspent" line to each budget, Fixed and Semi-Variable.

Overspent
When the Fixed Costs or Semi-Variable Costs exceed their budget, the budget will show a negative overage. If any budget is overspent, the company is not in balance.

Unspent
When either Fixed or Semi-Variable budgets have money left over after all expenses are paid, the budgets are underspent, leaving unspent funds. The unspent money is available at any moment for unexpected changes that might occur within the current year.

Fixed Expenses + UNSPENT = Fixed Budget.
Semi-Variable Expenses + UNSPENT = Semi-Variable Budget.

Update the Budget One Time Per Year
Fixed and Semi-Variable Costs can be different each year. Kanketa recommends only revising the budget once a year at the beginning of the new calendar or fiscal year of the business. When you separate all your monthly Non-People Costs into Fixed and Semi-Variable expense categories, you might find more costs on one side or the other. You should do everything possible to balance them out. This typically does not happen immediately, but there are many ways to get this to happen over time.

Some expenses might be Fixed Costs one year, such as a monthly legal or accounting retainer that can be negotiated to a Semi-Variable payment as needed the next year. At 100% Normal sales levels the business is in balance when Fixed Costs equal Semi-Variable Costs, and People Costs equal Non-People Costs.

Both Fixed and Semi-Variable budgets have a category in place for unspent money. Any unspent money that is not used for unexpected changes that might occur within the current year becomes a contribution to Net Profit at midnight of the last day of the month.

True Story: Semi-Variable Honesty Always Wins

Colin's Engineering firm of 17 employees was the bright star in Des Moines, Iowa. Colin did everything imaginable to hire the best and the brightest minds in the business. He recruited and imported from anywhere and everywhere at any expense. He paid top dollar and made sure that every engineer was given all the benefits. Colin's philosophy was "You get what you pay for." People were his highest expense. He built the entire reputation of his firm on the experience and quality of his engineers. He believed that if he paid extremely well, nobody would leave.

Then, in 2008, the economy took a turn for the worst. Cashflow became difficult. Colin found himself at the bank borrowing salaries on a routine basis. His engineers were oblivious to the firm's problems and went on with their days in comfort. Finally, Colin's credit ran dry. He was faced with the bitter truth and called the team together to discuss the condition of the company and announce layoffs.

When his employees heard this, they were angry. The ringleader who usually represented the group spoke out.

"Why didn't you tell us that this was happening? We would have much preferred being paid according to how well the company was performing than lose our jobs altogether."

Honesty and transparency are always the best policy when dealing with employees. You will lose them when you lose their trust. Offer performance compensation at the time of hire.

Offer one-half of the compensation as a Fixed salary for maintaining the profitability of the position. Offer one-half of the compensation as Semi-Variable performance compensation for growing the profitability of the position. When the company does well, everyone does well.

Balance your People Costs in the Margin (manager compensation) ... **with your Non-People overhead expenses.**

In other words, Financial Balance is

your budgeted Fixed Cost items plus any remaining unspent Fixed Cost amount, and your budgeted Semi-Variable Costs plus any remaining unspent Semi-Variable Cost amount.

In this way, as costs fluctuate in the year, you do not have to completely re-budget and you always have money to pay your bills.

Adjusting Your Budget Without Re-Budgeting

To manage small fluctuations that occur throughout the year, simply adjust your smaller costs in each budget by using up any unspent costs.

Let's say that your Fixed Non-People Costs include a cellphone contract of $200 a month. Your Fixed Costs budget for all contracted services has $500 budgeted but $300 is still unspent. You want to add another employee to your cellphone contract for $100.

Take $100 from your Unspent Fixed Non-People Cost budget and add it to your cell phone contract. Your cellphone contract is adjusted to $300. Your remaining unspent budget is now $400. At any time, you may adjust your Fixed budget without increasing it for the year. Incidentally, these are all monthly expenses. Large companies usually manage their budgets by the quarter. But all Kanketa small businesses strictly manage by the month.

BALANCE FIXED & SEMI-VARIABLE NON-PEOPLE

**People budgets are negotiable and easier to balance.
Non-People budgets, not so much.**

This is a graphic illustration of the Non-People budget in balance at Normal
sales levels. On the LEFT side are the Non-People Fixed Costs. The RIGHT
side holds the Non-People Semi-Variable Costs.

Example: NON-PEOPLE BUDGET $6,000

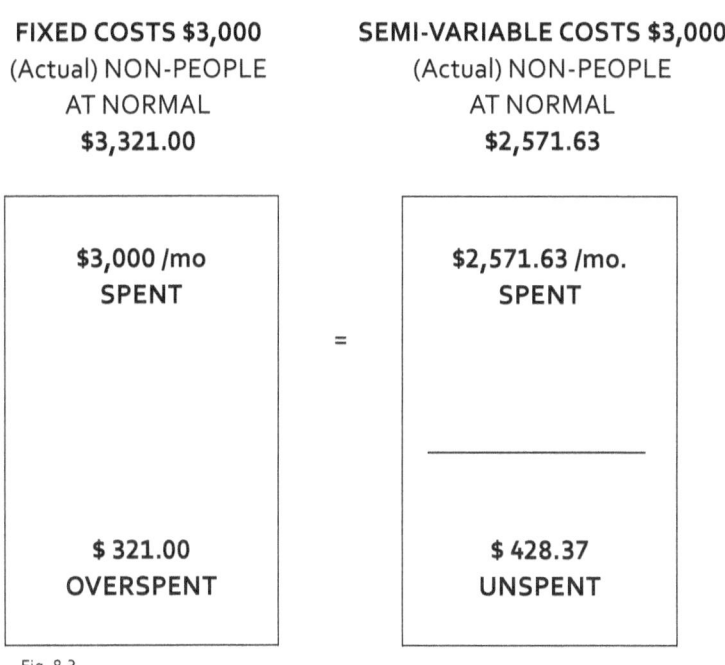

FIXED COSTS $3,000	SEMI-VARIABLE COSTS $3,000
(Actual) NON-PEOPLE	(Actual) NON-PEOPLE
AT NORMAL	AT NORMAL
$3,321.00	**$2,571.63**

$3,000 /mo SPENT	=	$2,571.63 /mo. SPENT
$ 321.00 OVERSPENT		**$ 428.37 UNSPENT**

Fig. 8.3

In this example, at 100% Normal, the Non-People Costs of $6,000 would
be equally divided into $3,000 Fixed Non-People Costs and $3,000 Semi-
Variable Non-People Costs. You must always keep exploring different ways
to balance your budget by constantly asking yourself ...

What can I **negotiate?**

What can I **combine?**

What can I **eliminate?**

What can I **outsource?**

What can I **rethink?**

What can I **reassign?**

As you create your budget in this manner, you will find that one and/or both expense sides (Fixed or Semi-Variable Costs) might have an UNSPENT amount of money. You might also find that one of the sides has a NEGATIVE, or OVERSPENT amount.

When either the Fixed Non-People Cost category, or the Semi-Variable Non-People expenses category have money left over after all expenses are budgeted, that category should show the UNSPENT amount. Unspent can be used any time during the year for unexpected surprises as long as the unspent money remains is used for items within its Fixed or Semi-Variable category.

Budget Overruns

When one side's expenses have a cost overrun and the Fixed or Semi-Variable Costs exceed the budget, that side should show a NEGATIVE or UNSPENT amount.

An unspent part of the budget does not affect the company's balance but, the budget is not in balance when one of the two operational budgets (Fixed or Semi-Variable) exceeds the other.

DIFFERENT WAYS TO SAY THE SAME THING

From time to time, you might find it useful to express your budget as the balance between People Costs (managers) and Non-People Costs (operational overhead). Your Balanced Budget is Fixed Costs equal to Semi-Variable Costs at Normal. But your Balanced Budget can also be People Costs balanced with Non-People Costs at Normal. It's the same difference.

GROSS SALES at Normal		GROSS SALES at Normal	
- Cost of Goods Sold		– Cost of Goods Sold	
= MARGIN		= MARGIN	
PEOPLE (managers)	$24,000	FIXED COSTS	$24,000
Fixed salaries	$12,000	Fixed People Costs	$12,000
Semi-Variable Performance Compensation		Fixed Non-People Costs	
	$12,000		$12,000
NON-PEOPLE (Operating overhead)		SEMI-VARIABLE COSTS	
	$24,000		$24,000
		Semi-Variable People Costs	
Fixed Operating Costs	$12,000		$12,000
Semi-Variable Operating Costs	$12,000	Semi-Variable Non-People Costs	$12,000
NET PROFIT	$24,000	NET PROFIT	$24,000

> The balance between People and Non-People is the same number as the balance between Fixed and Semi-Variable Costs. When calculating Net Profit, they are interchangeable.

"FIX IT. DON'T MIX IT!"

Never pay for negative costs
in one section of the budget with

EXCESS MONEY
in another section

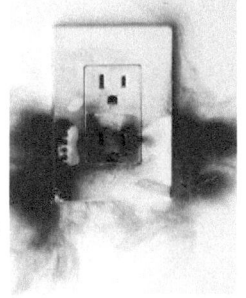

A big temptation for every business owner is to "rob Peter to pay Paul". It might be convenient for a busy owner to take money from one side of the budget to fix the other, but it plays havoc when it comes to business safety.

This practice of comingling hurts the company in the long run. When you borrow much needed money from the sales budget to pay rent, you are compromising your sales pipeline. When you borrow Semi-Variable car allowances to pay for Fixed insurance premiums, you find yourself visiting your customers less. When you borrow from Cost of Goods Sold to pay for operating costs, you're in jail (Cost of Goods Sold is not your money).

Fix the problem with better budgeting, planning and negotiating. Use your Line of Credit in the way it is intended. If you don't, you will have a hodge-podge of costs that will become uncontrollable. In other words, fix it, don't mix it.

The critical balance happens between Fixed Costs (costs that do not change from month to month) and Semi-Variable Costs (costs that do change slightly from month to month by 10% as sales levels increase or decrease).

> **Fix it. Don't Mix it.**
> Never pay for an overspent (negative) part of the budget on one side of the budget with unspent money from the other side. Never, ever use Cost of Goods Sold money for anything other than Cost of Goods Sold

ALWAYS WORK TO ADJUST...

YOUR FIXED EXPENSES + Unspent
and YOUR SEMI-VARIABLE EXPENSES + Unspent

TO BE EQUAL

Constantly ask yourself ...

"What costs in one section can be negotiated to put the costs into the other section to achieve a better balance?"

"What costs can be combined?"

"What costs can be eliminated or avoided?"

"What costs can be reduced?"

"What costs can be outsourced?"

"What costs can be redesigned, or re-engineered?"

"What costs can be reassigned?"

Make this your money mantra. Do this constantly. Over and over.

It's all about moving expenses from one side to the other to achieve balance.

Take your time with this. Semi-Variable costing will be the key that unlocks the maximum profitability in your business.

The goal is to get your Margin to be balanced at Normal.

True Story: Fix it. Don't Mix it.

The machine shop of Jeremy and Brad in Tucson, Arizona was always on the fence. Over the years they developed a bad habit of mixing budgets. When they would replace a copier in need of repair by borrowing from the money that was budgeted for a new salesperson. They paid for inadequate production space from their customer service budget. They borrowed sales money to pay for delivery from dissatisfied customers. In short, they constantly robbed from both Peter and Paul to pay for some answer that never materialized. Their reasons were always justified by a just-around-the corner sure thing return on investment that was certain to replace the money quickly. The problem escalated when the investments didn't work out as planned.

Finally, they received an offer from a large potential customer. The customer would require more service people than Brad and Jeremy could afford. Unfortunately, the two used the service budget for other things. The customer was not willing to front the machine shop and the customer's opportunity evaporated.

Instead of focusing on better and different possible solutions for the budget insufficiencies and protecting the budget balance, they ignored and upset the critical balance that they needed for long term stability and growth. Had the machine shop kept the budgets separate, they would have been able to take on the new customer who would have paid them enough to fill the financial voids.

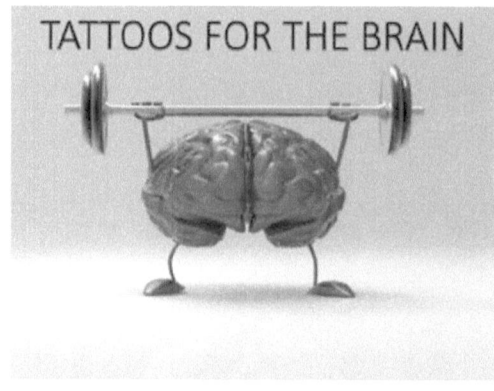

THREE SEMI-VARIABLE TATTOOS FOR THE BRAIN

Here are three main takeaways for the Semi-Variable Costs of a Kanketa Balanced Budget.

#1. Semi-Variable Costs are the backbone of a Balanced Budget. Without Semi-Variable Costs, there is no balance.

#2. Semi-Variable Costs are measured and budgeted in ten percent increments.

#3. Semi-Variable Cost items can be renegotiated from year to year to become Fixed Costs.

MONEY KEPT

All the money that
the owner invests in the business
that is used to grow the company
after monthly operating expenses

Net Profit for later.

CHAPTER 9

BUDGET PART 6 of 6

NET PROFIT FOR REINVESTMENT
To Keep Your Business Competitive

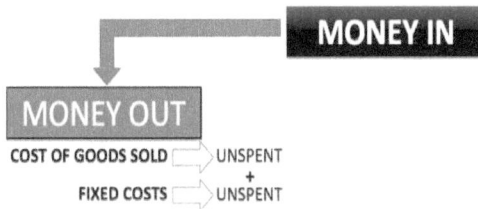

THE KANKETA PROFIT PLAN

In a high-performing company, Net Profit demands the same balance as all other costs.

Without a defined, written plan, an imbalanced use of Net Profit will result.

It's great if you are making a profit in your business. Hats off to you. So, exactly what do you keep of what you've earned and what do you do with it?

You keep what you don't spend after you have paid all your expenses.

"Duh, OK, so what's new?" you ask.

The goal for creating Net Profit in a high-performing company is

❖ Consistency

❖ Predictability

❖ Repeatability

❖ Sustainability

❖ Reliability

These goals are not only possible; they are business as usual in Kanketa companies.

Consider this. Toyota had three devastating recalls of hundreds of thousands of vehicles. A month later Japan suffered a tsunami that crippled one-third of the country. With no government bailout loans, and no employees let go or workforce reduction as a result, why was Toyota in a financial position to show up a week later and advertise aggressively on the Super Bowl like nothing happened?

This is because, in a sense, nothing much did happen to Toyota's business. Toyota operates profitably ... always in balance.

NET PROFIT WITHOUT A PLAN

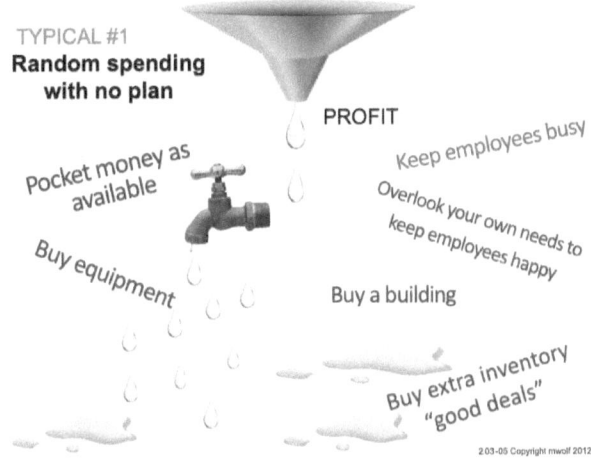

TYPICAL #1
Random spending with no plan

PROFIT

Pocket money as available

Keep employees busy

Overlook your own needs to keep employees happy

Buy equipment

Buy a building

Buy extra inventory "good deals"

2.03-05 Copyright mwolf 2012

Most of the small business owners I've seen rarely have a concisely followed plan for their profit. Many predictably spend their Net Profit on something unpredictable – often the next shiny object that lands in their path.

NET PROFIT WITH A POOR PLAN

Net Profit can all too easily be an emotional spend. This is usually because small business owners (more predominantly in the U.S.) who are constantly under the pressure of handling day-to-day problems feel that their business owes them. The emotional spending is done without much planning, often in wrong amounts for the wrong reasons. After all, look at all the choices we have for absolutely everything. Choices are fogging up our windshield. We Americans have so much that is so easily accessible, it is becoming impossible to discern the difference between needs and wants, and the value of later vs. must have now.

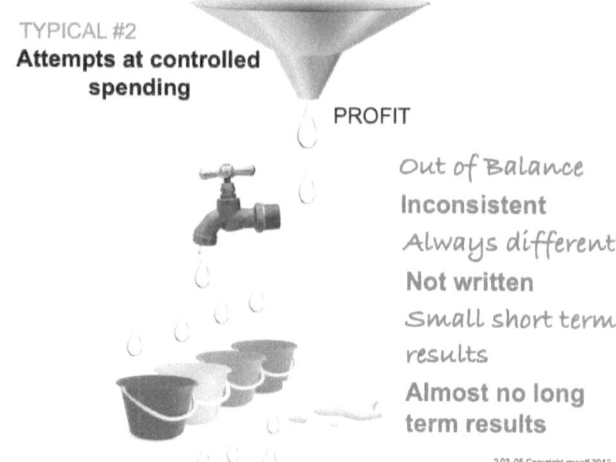

CALCULATING NET PROFIT
IN A BALANCED BUDGET

"How much Net Profit should I make? What's reasonable?"

THE CONCEPT OF SEMI-VARIABLE DOES NOT APPLY TO NET PROFIT. NET PROFIT IS NOT CALCULATED AS A PERCENT OF NORMAL.

When calculating Net Profit, subtract Fixed Costs and Semi-Variable Costs from the month's performance Margin. Net Profit can also be calculated by subtracting People Costs and Non-People Costs from the Margin. I said earlier that in a Balanced Budget, these cost types are interchangeable.

The Margin of a company in balance has 50% Fixed Costs (spent and unspent), and 50% Semi-Variable Costs (spent and unspent).

The Margin of a company in balance has 50% People Cost (spent and unspent), and 50% Non-People Costs (spent and unspent).

It is critical to always remember that the Semi-Variable Cost 10% increase or decrease only applies to operating overhead (employees, and operating costs).

CAUTION:

The concept of 10% Semi-Variable increments does **NOT** apply to Net Profit. If a company performs at 70% of Normal in a month, the Net Profit IS NOT 70% of Net Profit at Normal

when either Fixed or Semi-Variable Costs are subtracted from the Performance Margin of the month...

or when People Costs and Non-People Costs are subtracted from the Performance Margin of the month.

4 COMPONENTS OF A THE KANKETA

NET PROFIT BUDGET

> The concept of Semi-Variable
> does not apply to Net Profit.
> Net Profit is calculated by subtraction.
> Net Profit is not a percentage of Normal

Begin with the four main Net Profit buckets. Divide each equally.

NET PROFIT

25% REINVEST short - long

25% RETAIN short - long

25% TAXES short - long

25% SHAREHOLDERS short - long

Never stop reinvesting into your own business. You will always get a better return on your money than from the stock market. However, only invest what you can afford when you can afford it without jeopardizing the other budgets. Your monthly reinvestment budget should not exceed 25% of your total Net Profit.

12.5% Short-term reinvestment – 12 months or less is the expected timeframe that the return on investment should come back to the owner at 3:1 ($3 returned for every dollar invested).

12.5% Long-term reinvestment – 13 months or more is the expected timeframe that the return on investment should come back to the owner at 3:1 ($3 returned for every dollar invested).

SAVE 25% OF YOUR NET PROFIT
RETAINED EARNINGS
Keep your Company Safe

Building your corporate savings account is critical to your long-term success for different reasons than you might think. This is the safety money in your business. What you must be aware of is how your customers are borrowing your safety money interest free (accounts receivable) to run their business. They prefer your financing over having to go to the bank themselves.

12.5% Short-term Retained Earnings – 12 months or less is the expected timeframe that the profit is used to support potential business problems such as bad debts and business interruptions.

12.5% Long-term Retained Earnings – 13 months or more is the expected timeframe that the profit is used to support unforeseen emergencies.

25% Short-term Tax payments – 12 months or less. The Net Profit from each month builds the corporate tax savings account. On the average, save 17% of Net Profit for federal corporate tax. On the average, save 8% of Net Profit for state corporate tax.

12.5% Shareholder Disbursements – pays Shareholders for the current month.

12.5% is a suggested quarterly distribution.

True Story: Bankrupting with Generosity

Gaylan wanted to reward the employees of his outdoor sporting equipment shop in Dundee, Illinois. He awarded them with stock in the company because they worked hard.

At the end of the year, his intended generosity worked against him. The company wound up at 70% of Normal and the Shareholder Net Profit was very small. Instead of cheers of appreciation, the employees complained. Eventually, they were so disappointed that they banded together and took over Gaylan's company.

It's simple mathematics, and even simpler logic.

DON'T give any employee shares in your company if you can help it. Give them profit-sharing above Normal, which is the only time you can afford it.

DON'T award any employee with shares because they work hard. You are already paying them to work hard and they earn Semi-Variable Performance Compensation for working hard.

If you must give shares (for reasons I am unaware of), don't award more than 19% to any single person. Any employee with less than 20% is not considered a significant Shareholder.

Only Shareholders with 20% shares or more are considered by banks to be business owners. These are the only acceptable signatures on loans and bank documents.

Short-term reinvestment implies that whatever Net Profit is being used is fully returned to the owner before the end of the current year. While reinvestment can be for anything, marketing and sales are the focus here since this is the primary use of these funds.

"What should I budget for marketing?"

My answer is in two parts.

First-time Marketing Initiative

For any new, first-time marketing initiative such as a website, signage, displays, radio/tv, or the creation of any media, you should not budget more than .0417 (4.17%) of your yearly Normal Margin. If your Margin is $60,000 a month, then your first-time marketing should not exceed $60,000 multiplied by 12 months = $720,00 X .0417 or $30,000 for the year.

Why? Because this is the total amount of Net Profit that you can afford to reinvest to grow your company. I will give you examples in this chapter. If you invest more than this, your company for new marketing projects is out of balance and becomes unsafe.

How do you plan to increase Net Sales this year by 20%? What resources do you need to do this?

Consider your manpower, methods, machines, measurements, milieu (workspace), MTP (most-trusted partner-suppliers), materials, and most importantly of all, the mindset of your team. Do they need coaching and training?

Do you need a new website or marketing media or materials for a market that you are not in yet? Will you need to establish a new line of inventory that is not currently in place?

Your travel budget is not a reinvestment, but an ongoing expense separately treated in your Non-People budget with the exception of a one-time major conference or event.

Monthly Marketing Maintenance

Additional reoccurring marketing maintenance costs after the first-time marketing initiative are not part of reinvestment. Marketing maintenance is part of your Non-People Fixed Cost budget. If a balanced budget is your goal, marketing maintenance should not exceed .0417 (4.17%) of your Normal Monthly Margin.

In Kanketa, your marketing maintenance is considered a Fixed Cost. When your sales are low, you must spend a minimum for marketing to maintain your customer volume. When your sales are high, you must spend a maximum for marketing to grow your business and increase your Normal by 20%. The Retained Earnings part of your profit is designed to support your marketing maintenance effort no matter what condition you are in.

Short-Term Reinvestment
SUMMARY

Budget 12.5% of annual Net Profit at Normal to be used for reinvestment for short-term business growth. Return on investment: 12 months or less.

Types of short-term reinvestments:

- Cashflow loan to the business as a line of credit
- First-time marketing initiatives (a website, wearables, radio /tv production, etc.)
- A new hire who is not yet productive
- Purchased inventory that will turn within 12 months
- Payments for a small-asset purchase (printer, office equipment)
- Payments for a one-time start up or set up of office services
- One-time software purchase (accounting software, application software)
- Repaying a short-term bank loan – 12 months or less
- Unexpected, unforeseen short-term opportunities (costs to rescue customers of a competitor who goes out of business)

<u>REINVESTMENTS ARE NOT INTENDED TO PAY FOR MONTHLY FIXED, RECURRING OPERATIONAL EXPENSES.</u>

Kanketa minimum expectations of reinvestment: $3 returned to the owner for every dollar invested

- $1 returns the original dollar that was invested
- $1 returns the profit on the dollar for the risk of the investment
- $1 pays for the owner's time to get involved with the investment (conversations about the re-investment, time to manage the re-investment)

As a long-term reinvestment, your monthly payments should not exceed 12.5% of Net Profit at Normal. Any long-term reinvestment into the business is technically always paying the debt as it is incurred. Reinvestment is intended for business growth and not intended for paying back debts.

Ideally, you would plan your reinvestments for the new year once a year within the first week or so when you establish your new budget. Because the new year is based on what you did in the year prior, you already know what your reinvestment budget is and can plan accordingly.

Long-Term Reinvestment
SUMMARY

Budget 12.5% of annual Net Profit at Normal to be used for reinvestment for long-term business growth. Return on investment: 13 months or more.

Types of long-term reinvestment:

- Payments (principal only) for a large asset purchase (vehicle or large equipment)
- Amortized payments to pave a driveway, repair a roof
- Invest in another business
- Payments for long-term financing (SBA 10 year term loan, etc.)

REINVESTMENTS DO NOT PAY FOR MONTHLY FIXED, RECURRING OPERATIONAL EXPENSES

(Monthly long-term leases are in Fixed Non-People Costs.)

"What should I pay toward debt reduction?"

Retained Earnings is money kept in the company and not disbursed. Kanketa puts aside short-term and long-term money into savings to ensure business safety in the event of an unforeseen situation (positive or negative).

"How much debt can I afford to have?"

Let's take a hard look at debt.

Goal of Debt Reduction:
Reduce your debt to be equal to or less than your NORMAL MONTHLY MARGIN.

How much credit do you plan to allow for all customers combined? Many larger customers will try to make you their bank because they think they can. But you are not a bank, and providing a banking service for your customers is not be the business you are in.

Make your credit policies known to all customers and hold the line. If they try to bully you, and you are having a difficult time with this, then borrow the credit amount that you are extending to them and charge them a higher interest than you are paying. If you don't do this, you will have cashflow problems and eventually you could go broke.

There are three unsafe conditions that Retained Earnings are designed to cover:

1. Unexpected situations that might interrupt the growth and health of the business, such as an unexpected competitor move, an unforeseen change in the marketplace, i.e. a social, technological, economic, environmental, political, ethical or demographic change that could interrupt the business quickly, etc.

2. Expected situations such as late customer payments that extend beyond 30 days (credit that you extend to your customers) and bad debts.

3. Late bills beyond 30 days due to creditors.

"How much should we allow for accounts receivable?"

"Tripwire Credit" is the maximum credit that you can afford to give to all customers combined. Trip wire credit is your point of putting your customers on credit hold before using your company's safety to keep them in balance while they throw you out of balance.

Tripwire credit is half of the annual Retained Earnings budget at Normal.

One approach is to allow 60% of your trip wire credit to all customers combined who pay in more than 30 but within 45 days. These people combined are allowed half of Retained Earnings at Normal times 60%.

The folks who pay later than 45 days, but in less than 60 days, share 25% of your trip wire total. And finally, the real delinquents above 61 days share the final 15%.

The bottom line of Tripwire credit: Don't give more than ½ of your Normal Monthly Margin as credit to all customers combined (the same as .0417 X Normal Monthly Margin X 12 months).

True Story: Tripping over the Tripwire

Ted's distributing business in Pittsburgh sold audio gear, small electronics, recording boards, meters, attenuators, etc. Ted supplied 110 dealers. The company billed $150,000 a month. He had dealers of all sizes. Twelve were large dealers, representing about 65% of his business, 45 mid-sized dealers that were 20% of sales and the rest were small occasional dealers who made up the remaining 15%.

Ted had a 40% Margin of $60,000 a month after Cost of Goods Sold. Ted's business was not in balance. While his Net Profit was typically $15,000 a month, he didn't budget or manage the profit well. He was very reactionary in his spending habits and paid the loudest screaming suppliers first. His large customers were slow to pay, taking 45 to 75 days to pay for orders. Ted was afraid to demand stricter payment terms. As his large customers grew, he kept extending credit to match their growth. Finally, his banking relationships became strained and he mortgaged his house, his car and spent part of his son's college fund to fund his inventory.

Ted's accounts receivable was over $230,000 and over half of the receivables slid into 120 to 160 days overdue. Eventually he had to rely on high risk high interest lenders for his inventory. Soon, he found himself doing routine loan and debt consolidations. He was no longer borrowing for inventory. He was always borrowing to pay off the previous loans. The interest on his loans became 18%, 20%, 25% and more which exceeded the average 12% Net Profit of the company. Finally, his Net Profit was insufficient to keep up with the loans and he had to get investors. After nine years of being in his own business, he ended up working as employee for the investors, who later sold the company. Ted was laid off.

Had Ted's monthly total loan payments for inventory not exceeded 12.5% of his Net Profit for all customers combined (the same as .0417 X $60,000 - his monthly Margin at Normal - X 12 months), his business would have grown at the same rate as his customers. He should also have factored the receivables and charged his customers the factoring interest in the price.

Short-Term Retained Earnings
SUMMARY

RETAINED EARNINGS – Short

Budget 12.5% of annual Net Profit at Normal to be deposited into savings for short-term business stability - 12 months or less.

Types of savings purposes:

- Credit to customers who are slow payers. Pays for factoring costs.
- Funds receivables 31-89 days.
- Supports unexpected short-term dip in sales.
- Unexpected, unforeseen short-term changes to your company (absenteeism due to employee health issues, small damages to property, etc.)

RETAINED EARNINGS AND SAVINGS ARE NOT USED FOR MONTHLY RECURRING OPERATIONAL EXPENSES.

Long-Term Retained Earnings
SUMMARY

Budget 12.5% of annual Net Profit at Normal to be deposited into savings for long-term business stability - 12 months or less.

Reasons for saving:

- Bad debts
- Unexpected, unforeseen changes in the industry that need immediate response, i.e. competitor moves, product obsolescence, vendors or customers going out of business, etc.
- Social, technological, environmental, economic, political legal, ethical and demographic changes of age, education and income changes.
- Unexpected, unforeseen long-term changes to your company (death, incapacitation, disability, permanent absenteeism, large damages to property, etc.).
- Exit of the owner.
- May also be used for general debt reduction.

RETAINED EARNINGS AND SAVINGS ARE NOT USED FOR MONTHLY RECURRING OPERATIONAL EXPENSES.

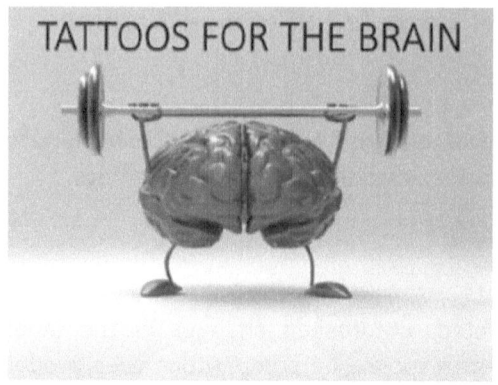

TATTOOS FOR THE BRAIN

<u>THREE NET PROFIT TATTOOS FOR THE BRAIN</u>

Here are three main takeaways for money kept in a Kanketa Balanced Budget.

#1. Money Kept is not profit kept.

#2. Money Kept is predictable, sustainable and its components maintain a balance.

#3. Money Kept alone does not create personal financial freedom. It is the first step.

MONEY MANAGED

All money that

the owner does not personally

take as a dividend

that is used to keep the company

safe and growing

Net Profit for later.

Managing Your Money

As with the ownership of anything of value, the owner of a business has a choice to use the Net Profit of the business to reinvest in the company's short-term and long-term growth, and to protect the business from the unforeseen changes that occur. I am not suggesting that the owner must or must not do anything. It's simply about choices for managing money properly and the outcomes of doing so or not doing so... without judgement.

In all the businesses that I've worked with, there are four questions that universally keep rising to the top from their owners. Unfortunately, these business owners have usually not read these pages when the questions are posed, and I rarely have the time to properly and thoroughly explain my responses. Sometimes, my replies might come off rather short. Nonetheless, I can't dance around the best answers. It's all math. The math has been proven over decades. The answers can be found in this book.

Managing money includes managing your own money as well as another peoples' money. Until you learn how to become your own bank and pay yourself more interest than investing your money in the stock market (a sequel I'm writing), there is a good chance that you must rely on outside money sources to keep your business safe. The question becomes... exactly how much money do you need, and for what purposes?

NECESSARY LINE OF CREDIT

"What should I have for a line of credit?"

Normal Monthly Margin multiplied by 1.8 is the maximum amount of money needed to operate your company every month. If you need more than this, you are probably not managing your expenses efficiently.

YOUR BUSINESS CHECKBOOK BALANCE

"What balance should I keep in the business checking account?"

What should your total balance be in all checking accounts that the business maintains? Normal Monthly Margin multiplied by .67 is the ideal total amount of money that should always be in your accounts.

A GOOD MONTHLY TARGET FOR SAVINGS

"How much should I have in corporate savings?"

Normal Monthly Margin X 4 X .67 is the ideal amount of money needed to keep your company safe from unexpected turbulence. This is a target amount that will take time to build. A minimum of 25% of your Net Profit should be deposited every month into savings. One-half of this Net Profit (12.5% of all Net Profit) shouldn't be touched until the last day of the year. The other half should be available to fund all accounts receivable between 31 and 89 days (or to fund the total of your merchant cash advances if you are a retailer).

MAXIMUM CREDIT AVAILABLE TO YOUR CUSTOMERS

"How much credit should I give to my customers?"

Review:

How much credit should you give to all of your customers combined at any one time? This amount is called "Tripwire Credit". Fifty percent of Normal Monthly Margin is the maximum amount of credit beyond 30 days that a financially safe company can afford to give to all customers combined.

CHAPTER 10

SHADEHOLDERS
NET PROFIT
INCLUDES CORPORATE TAXES

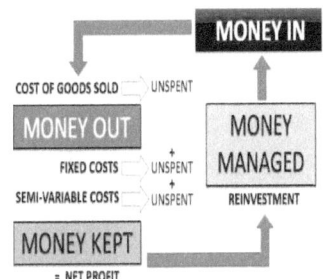

In Kanketa, Net Profit consists of four equal parts:

1. Money to reinvest into your business to stay competitive

2. Money to put into savings for unforeseen circumstances (business interruptions or opportunities)

3. Money for corporate taxes (federal and state)

4. Money for you, the business owner

Net Profit is the only place in the Kanketa system where the word "Profit" is used. Net Profit is what remains of the Margin after all Fixed Costs and Semi-Variable Costs are paid. At least this is what we have been taught.

Western business builds budgets from the top down. Kanketa builds budgets from the bottom up. When you put the owner first, the company is really in the first position.

If I were to ask you, "How much should, would, could your business pay you every single month for not showing up while your business continues to grow without you?", what would your answer be? Isn't your answer the real reason for owning your business? I will answer this question in the pages to follow.

Certainly, there are a million different reasons to be in your own business. But eventually you will have to sell it, lease it, close it, will it to the family, or give it away. And when you do, it will always come down to money and business value.

America is the only place in the world where it takes more brains to make out an income tax return than it does to make the income. There are some simple, safe ways to monitor and manage corporate taxes.

"What should I save for corporate taxes?"

These are corporate taxes for taxable types of companies, such as a C Corporation. These are also saved for taxes of owners of Sub-S Corporations, Limited Liability Companies, and Sole Proprietorships.

Net Profit for Now

Each month, a diligent business owner should routinely put 25% of the month's Net Profit away for year-end corporate taxes (state and federal). Certainly, whatever taxes are not due at the end of the year are returned to the owner.

Safely, I suggest that you save 17% of your Net Profit for federal corporate tax and 8% for state corporate tax, for a total of 25% of the Net Profit of your business.

Do not use this budget to pay back taxes. Delinquencies, tax penalties and interest on taxes are paid out of debt payments from long-term Retained Earnings. If your state does not charge corporate tax, save it anyway. There are plenty of reasons for this and ways to use this money to reduce your tax liability overall. Taxes are based on supply and demand. The government demands, and we supply. The Kanketa "Quadra-Structure," offers many ways to legally control and avoid some of these taxes. For now, these guidelines are sufficient. They are safe amounts for any accountant.

You might find it quite advantageous to expand your business when your state corporate taxes are more than $1,700 a year. There are significant tax advantages for this type of expansion. For information on this, submit your request to info@kanketa.com.

TAX MANAGEMENT

Every business owner falls into two categories of tax management: RESOLUTION and REDUCTION. For decades I have <u>always</u> found every tax return to be in at least one, if not several, of the following conditions:

- *OVERPAID*

The taxpayer followed some software instructions and paid taxes accordingly because "it said so." After all, the evidence is right there on the screen. Certainly, that can't be wrong. It instructs millions of users (QuickBooks, TurboTax, Quicken, H&R Block, Tax Act, etc.).

These software systems aren't wrong. They are designed to correctly push volumes of "patients" through the tax hoop based on a set of laws that are good for the goose and the gander. It's no different than the medical profession. Two over-the-counter pills in a 95-pound person over the age of 12 produces an overdose while a 300 lb. 70-year-old has minimal effect as the condition persists.

- *INCORRECT*

There are always errors in returns of people who do it themselves. Wrong numbers in right places, or right numbers in wrong places all add up to the same thing.

- *INACCURATE*

With 9 million words in the U.S. tax code (7 bibles) and 20% of the them changing every year, nearly every tax return is inaccurately calculated. Business owners just want to get it off their plate.

- *MISGUIDED*

Everyone has their favorite accountant who makes them feel safe and secure. And every accountant is trained to fill out government forms and give tax advice. The problem becomes the limitation in the training offered. While everyone must do file-your-taxes 101, there are several levels of accounting certifications and licenses available to bookkeepers, accountants, tax attorneys, certified public accountants, etc. They will each guide you to their corner for a fee.

- *UNJUSTLY TREATED*

The overwhelmed IRS collection agency is processing what comes and computers are doing the processing. There is a high percentage of administrative processing errors that will not be addressed unless the taxpayer is able to find it, understand it, and bring it to someone's attention in a way that makes sense to the agent on the phone within their three-minute conversation allowance.

- *MISHANDLED*

Professional tax preparers are human. They do guesswork and are often guilty of not following through. The taxpayer who is pinched between a negligent tax preparer and the stubborn IRS always loses. It often takes years and money to straighten out the smallest mishandled mistakes of a negligent tax preparer.

- *UNFILED*

Too busy (or too afraid) to file are not acceptable excuses to the IRS as you already know. So, you remain frozen in your tracks and frustrated because your limbs don't move to act.

The Bottom Line to Tax Resolution:

Your business is most likely in one or more of these scenarios today. You don't know who to trust, you don't know why you should trust anyone, and you don't know what you need in the first place?

How am I doing? Am I reasonably close here?

RESOLUTION before REDUCTION (Tax Elimination)

The first request we make to anyone regarding their tax situation is to see their most recently filed tax return. This is the starting point and the current situation.

In my experience, the most highly trained, highly experienced professionals to assist in tax resolution are licensed enrolled agents (EA) for the IRS. Their license and position allow them certain privileges that CPAs and other tax practitioners do not have.

What to Do with Your Past Tax Filings

Have an enrolled IRS agent (EA) review your most recently filed tax return to assess any inequities. They should always find oversights and errors and can efficiently correct overpayments and issues of the past with amended tax returns. They can resolve all issues directly with the IRS. There is no need for you to be present. Any fees they might charge will always be much less than the money that they are able to recover.

REDUCTION (Tax Avoidance)

The IRS train doesn't stop. The next biggest business expense after Cost of Goods Sold is taxes. Untreated taxes can rob you of over one-third of your income. Therefore, you should be attentive to your tax situation.

From the moment that your last tax return was filed, your tax responsibilities continue. Under newly formed tax laws each year, your taxes will continue to mount. Starting with your next tax return you are subject to all the same problems mentioned.

Now that you are in the world of tax REDUCTION (during the time that your previous taxes are being handled), everything after that is your current tax position for upcoming filings. What will you need for you unfiled tax returns?

ACCURATE BANK STATEMENTS

Nothing can be filed until you have correct numbers to work with. This is accomplished with reconciled bank statements for EACH MONTH following the last tax return filed. Without reconciled bank statements, the tax specialists don't know what the deductible expenses are. Month-by-month, errors will pile on top of errors until your books are so twisted, they become unusable.

TAX REDUCTION HAPPENS MONTHLY (Not at the end of the year)

The tax laws constantly change. Every day-to-day business decision that you make affect your taxes in some way. Therefore, constant (monthly) auditing is the best practice. Just one good sales month can change everything.

The outcome of monthly monitoring with an enrolled agent is paying the least taxes by law while remaining completely compliant. A monthly or quarterly enrolled agent review is a low-cost yearly IRS insurance policy that every business should have.

IRS Compliance Insurance

If you want to carry IRS insurance, $285 a month on the average is the cheapest compliance insurance you can have to ensure total freedom from IRS problems. Call me if you need help with this or locating an EA.

- EXCELLENT ACCOUNTING PRACTICES MAKE TAX REDUCTION EASIER

Your accountant provides you with a P&L statement that should accurately verify your actual expenses against your budget. Your P&L should show you the details of your Fixed and Semi-Variable expenses and will be the biggest help toward keeping your company balanced.

By comparing your detailed expenses with your budget, you will be able to define, identify, locate, and qualify problems and request solutions from your tax specialist for upcoming and existing performance problems as they occur. Don't wait until the end of the month to see how bad things turned out.

RESOLUTION is legal tax recovery.

REDUCTION is legal tax avoidance.

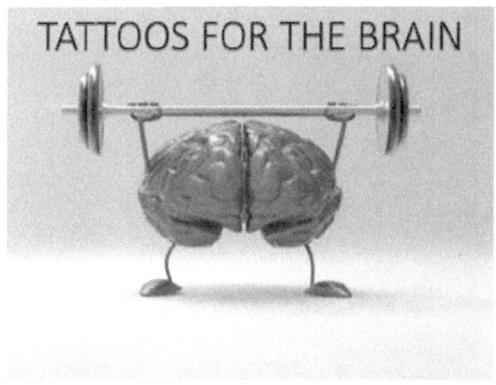

TATTOOS FOR THE BRAIN

THREE MONEY MANAGED TATTOOS FOR THE BRAIN

Here are three main takeaways for money kept in a Kanketa Balanced Budget.

#1. Tax avoidance is legal. Tax evasion is illegal.

#2. Save 17% of your Net Profit for federal corporate tax and 8% for state corporate tax for 25% of your Net Profit total.

#3. Hire a licensed IRS enrolled agent if you are looking for tax reduction. It's money well spent.

CHAPTER 11

CREATE A BALANCED BUDGET

"THAT'S A HORRIBLE IDEA.
WHEN DO WE START?"

The best time to start is yesterday. The next best time to start is today. Do not start unless it's a "hell, yes!". If it's not a "hell, yes!" then, it's a "hell, no!".

If you aren't absolutely convinced by now that this approach makes a whole lot of sense, don't go any further. I'm not suggesting that you shouldn't go slowly and carefully. I am suggesting that you should be deliberate. If you live by the belief that whatever got you to this point is no longer sufficient to keep you here, then, proceed vigorously with all determination.

Creating your balanced budget is in two parts.

PART 1: BUILD A P&L ORGANIZER. Organized expenses will aid in producing a balanced budget. This is a worksheet that either you can produce yourself on an Excel spreadsheet or request free at kanketa@kanketa.com.

PART 2: CREATE YOUR BALANCED BUDGET FROM YOUR ADJUSTED P&L.

PART 1: BUILD A P&L ORGANIZER

CREATING YOUR BALANCED BUDGET BEGINS BY ADJUSTING YOUR MOST CURRENT PROFIT AND LOSS STATEMENT

PRINT OUT YOUR LAST YEAR END (12-month) P&L

We will begin by breaking down your last year-end 12-month P&L into manageable, bitesize chunks. Since no P&L will already have the Kanketa balanced budget in place, we will initially use the standard GAAP system that already appears on your P&L to create the main budget sections that you will work with. Together, we will examine and work with each of 6 sections of your P&L statement, a section at a time.

ACCOUNT CODES

In this exercise, I will ask you to identify certain items on your P&L. If you identify anything incorrectly, it will negatively affect your short-term Net Profit, the short and long-term value of your company, and your tax liability for starters. Everything that you identify correctly will positively affect your short-term Net Profit, and the short and the long-term value of your company.

Please use account codes! They are good for business.

The first order of business is to obtain a Chart of Accounts. These account codes will help you to accurately categorize your main income and expenses. Your accountant might have their own account codes. If you are more comfortable with their codes, then by all means use them.

The account codes here are all that is necessary to achieve financial balance and make good day-to-day financial business decisions that keep your company safe. For our purposes here, we do not find it necessary to have more account codes than these. However, for your reasons, not ours, you might want to track other details about other sub-groups of expense items. If so, you should obtain and use the Chart of Accounts from your accountant.

KANKETA CHART OF ACCOUNTS
FOR A BALANCED BUDGET

INCOME

4101	Gross sales from customers for CORE products and services (that you produce)
4130	Gross sales from customers for BROKERED products and services (that you buy and resell)
4961	Uncategorized income (requires further verification)

COST OF QUALITY

5100	Samples
5120	Returned Items
5140	Discounts
5160	Warrantees
5180	Refunds and Costs for Errors Made
5190	Scrap
5191	Cost of Quality – Other

COST OF GOODS SOLD – Costs in the Job

5201	DIRECT LABOR (Individual Workers)
5310	SUPPLIES - Disposable Items Used in Jobs
5303	Materials for Resale
5320	Raw Materials - Manufacturing
5340	Packaging /Supplies and Services
5360	Merchandise (Ready to Use. Purchased for Resale)
5367	Services for Resale
5400	Commissions
5440	Direct Labor Benefits
5650	Rentals
5600	Contracted Services
5700	Shipping and Delivery
5750	Sales Tax
5752	Machine Parts and Equipment for Sale.
5753	Wearables, Uniforms for Protection and Cleanliness
5799	All Other Job Costs Not Listed

FIXED COSTS

6000   Manager Fixed Salaries
6200   Employee Benefits
6301   Advertising
6320   Insurances (Not Health)
6330   Contracts (monthly)
6340   Lease Payments - Equipment
6350   Lease /Rent Office
6351   Fixed Costs - Other

SEMI-VARIABLE COSTS

6001   Manager Performance Compensation
6400   Banking Services
6403   Credit Card Fees
6404   Interest
6405   Office Supplies
6410   Professional Fees
6420   Repairs, Maintenance (Not vehicles)
6430   Taxes (incl FUTA, FUTA, FICA matching) & business Licenses
6440   Vehicle - Operating (Gas Oil, Repairs, Parking, Car licenses)
6450   Travel and Per Diem (for Business)
6460   Meals and Entertainment (Customer)
6470   Utilities
6471   Semi-Variable Costs - Other

As we explore your last year's P&L, make your adjustments on your P&L and put the appropriate account codes next to each item. These account codes will help you to specifically identify various items and avoid costly accounting errors.

The account codes should give you clarity about potential errors and oversites on your P&L and offer hints as to how you might correct them. You will use the account codes to identify all income and expense items.

WHAT YOU WILL NEED

To organize your P&L and create a Balanced Budget you will need a few tools:

- A form or spreadsheet to organize your current P&L
- A Balanced Budget Worksheet for monthly use
- Chart of Account Codes
- Your mental presence

  Not in this order.

When you received this book, it came with my passion to help you and my pledge to give you everything you need to manage your money as accurately as possible.

Drop me a note at Kanketa@kanketa.com and request these. I will happily send you the additional easy-to-use electronic forms that you see here at absolutely no cost.

In case I do not hear from you, you may use a standard spreadsheet to create your own Kanketa Balanced Budget. In the following pages I will present the rows and columns that you will need to accomplish this. Either way will get you there.

Let's begin at the beginning, with income.

MONEY IN:

1. **Revenue**... which your P&L might show as income, is all the money that is deposited into your business checkbook. From your general revenue deposits, you must subtract any payments to you that do not come from customers and vendors (refunds, allowances, etc.).

Uncategorized Income

Essentially, there are only three kinds of revenue:

- Revenue that you clearly know is from products and services (Gross Sales)
- Revenue that you clearly know is NOT from the sale of products and services.
- Revenue that you are unsure about and must research further.

The revenue that you are unsure about might be temporarily labeled as "Uncategorized Income". If you have in categorized income, you should research those deposits to understand whether they were from customers for products and services. There should be no miscellaneous or unidentified items on your P&L. All uncategorized income should have an account code of **4961**.

1. **Gross Sales**

Your only concern for your business is the money that comes from customer payments for the purchase of products and services.

On your P&L, identify and locate the total Gross Sales last year for the sale of products and services. There are two main categories of business income:

4101 CORE Products and Services:

Deposits from products and services you produce

4130 BROKERED Products and Services:

Deposits from products and services that you buy for the purpose of resale

Using the two account codes for Gross Sales, notate the appropriate account code next to all income items on your P&L. When you have labeled every income item, add up the two Gross Sale groups of like account codes and transfer the totals of each to your P&L ORGANIZER (your form or mine).

On the P&L Organizer, identify and total the CORE products and services that you produced last year in the ADJUSTED ANNUAL column to the right of CORE PRODUCTS. Include SERVICES. Make any notes in the center "Description" column to generally describe your CORE PRODUCTS /SERVICES.

Identify and total BROKERED products and services that you bought and resold in the ADJUSTED ANNUAL column to the right of BROKERED PRODUCTS. Include SERVICES. Make any notes in the center column to generally describe your BROKERED PRODUCTS and SERVICES.

2. **Cost of Quality /Net Sales**

There are 6 primary Costs of Quality that I suggest you track and monitor.

> Samples (including costs for free surveys and assessments),
> Customer Product Returns and Restock,
> Discounts,
> Warranties & Gift Cards with Expiration Dates,
> Costs for your Error and Rework,
> and any unusable materials and items that you generally scrap.

You will have to pay for these costs now or later in some form or other.

ACCOUNT CODE	CURRENT FINANCIAL SITUATION DESCRIPTION	MONTHLY ADJUSTED P&L	ANNUAL ADJUSTED P&L
	TOTAL REVENUE PREVIOUS YEAR		
4961 Deposits Not from Customers			
	GROSS SALES		
4101 CORE PRODUCTS			
4130 BROKERED PRODUCTS			
	COST OF QUALITY		
5100 Samples			
5120 Returned Items			
5140 Discounts			
5160 Warranties			
5180 Error and Rework			
5190 Scrap			
	NET SALES		

Cost of Quality should have its own budget and its own checking account.

When you receive customer payments, leave the Cost of Quality budgeted amounts for these items in a dedicated checking account until they are no longer redeemable, such as a warranty. Another example is an expected, budgeted cost for error, waste and rework.

Ideally, Costs of Quality expense should be charged to a customer. Otherwise they are paid for out of the Net Profit of the business owner as a reinvestment.

My Own Cost of Quality

A free KANKETA P&L ORGANIZER form offered with this book.

As I said earlier, you may create your own on a spreadsheets and worksheets. But I'd like to offer you a Cost of Quality item that I have budgeted for and you have already paid for with my book: An already-coded, free P&L ORGANIZER and set of Budget Worksheets.

Send your request to info@kanketa.com. This is my "Free Samples" Cost of Quality.

Remember that your P&L is organized alphabetically for tax purposes. There is no intention for the government to give you any more P&L information about your business other than to show your tax liability.

Using your Cost of Quality Account Codes, identify and total the Cost of Quality items on your P&L. Put the total Cost of Quality amounts in the ADJUSTED ANNUAL box to the right and across from each Item. Make any notes in the center column to best describe the item or group of items.

Cost of Quality Description Example: Description for Discounts might be "10% off to the Military" or "100 warranties issued, good for 90 days at product value".

When you have located as many different Cost of Quality Items as possible on your P&L, group and total the costs for these items and enter them in the Annual Adjusted Cost of Quality column on the far right of your P&L Organizer. Enter the total Cost of Quality on the far right of the COST OF QUALITY row.

Net Sales

After subtracting Cost of Quality from your Gross Sales, you will have your Net Sales .... which are the total bank deposits that your business works with to pay its bills.

There are no standards for Cost of Quality. They will be different from industry to industry. Cost of Quality could be zero, although in our experience this is very rare.

3. Cost of Goods Sold

Cost of Goods Sold is the amount of money that is spent for job related production costs. These are subtracted from your Net Sales to give you your Gross Profit. You only have Cost of Goods Sold if you have the work to spend against. No job? No Cost of Goods Sold.

Using your Cost of Goods Sold account codes, identify and total the Cost of Goods items on your P&L. Make any descriptive notes (names of suppliers, types of items, etc.) in the center column to generally describe your Cost of Goods and Services.

Negative Numbers

Negative numbers mean that you owe that amount to someone, a customer, a vendor, an employee. Negative numbers should not be in your P&L. They are Balance Sheet items (what you own and what you owe).

Cost of Goods Sold Less Than 50% of Net Sales

When your Cost of Goods Sold exceeds 50% of Net Sales, your business is becoming unsafe. The more that Cost of Goods Sold exceeds your Margin, the more vulnerable you become. The goal is to have a Product/Service mix with a blended average of 50% Cost of Goods Sold or less.

COST OF GOODS SOLD	
5201 DIRECT LABOR (individuals)	
5301 Supplies (disposable)	
5303 Materials for Resale	
5320 Raw Materials (mfg)	
5340 Packaging (supplies & services)	
5360 Merchandise (for Resale)	
5367 Services (for Resale)	
5400 Commissions	
5440 Direct Labor Benefits	
5650 Rentals	
5600 Contracted Services (Companies)	
5700 Delivery & Shipping	
5750 Sales Tax	
5752 Equip Parts (mfg) Equip Resale	
5753 Uniforms, Wearables	
5799 Cost of Goods - OTHER	

NOTE:

5201 are the individual laborers that you hired to do the work.

5600 are the companies that you hired to do the work.

5752 is equipment that you bought and resold – regardless of the size, type, quantity or cost of the items. You might have bought and sold one piece of equipment in the entire year that cost you $100,000. Enter this piece as part of your Cost of Goods Sold.

5753 is wearables that you need for safety, protection and cleanliness in the execution of your job. These could be a uniform rental service that replaces wearables every month. These could be plastic suits in certain cases that give protection to beekeepers, basketball uniform cleaning or repair services after each game, or gloves for individuals who pick fruit and vegetables on farms.

The question is: Did a customer pay you for the job that required these items? If you have no work, would you need these items?

These are different than generally reusable advertising T-shirts for a law office with no specific job attached. That would come under the category of ADVERTISING.

IMPORTANT:

Because your P&L is nothing more than an alphabetical list of expenses, all of these costs are mixed together. You might find Cost of Quality items and Cost of Goods Sold scattered throughout the Gross Profit section of your P&L.

Kanketa refers to Gross Profit as "MARGIN".

MONEY OUT

Gross Profit on your P&L is all overhead costs to keep your business operating every month. The Margin – another word for Gross Profit, is for your overhead, the amount of money it takes every month to keep your doors open.

The Margin shows all operating expenses of your company.

In your P&L ORGANIZER, I will divide your MARGIN into 2 visually easier-to-manage sections.

4. **Fixed Overhead Costs (that do not change from month to month)**

	MARGIN	
	FIXED COSTS	
	FIXED PEOPLE COSTS	
6001 Manager Salaries		
	FIXED NON-PEOPLE COSTS	
6200 Employee Benefits		
6301 Advertising		
6320 Insurances (Not Health) Health Insurance is an Employee Benefit		
6330 Contracts (Monthly)		
6340 Lease Payments (Equipment)		
6350 Lease /Rent Office		
Fixed Other		

5. Semi-Variable Overhead Costs
(that do change from month to month)

	SEMI-VARIABLE COSTS	
	SEMI-VARIABLE PEOPLE COSTS	
6001 Manager Bonuses		☐
	SEMI-VARIABLE NON-PEOPLE COSTS	☐
6400 Banking Services		☐
6403 Credit Card Fees		☐
6404 Interest		☐
6405 Office Supplies		☐
6410 Professional Services		☐
6420 Repairs and Maintenance (Not Vehicles)		☐
6430 Taxes, Business Licenses includes FUTA, SUTA, FICA matching		☐
6440 Vehicles - All Expenses Vehicle Operation	Gas, Oil, Maintenance, Plates, Permits	☐
6450 Travel, Per Diem for Business Customers, Suppliers		☐
6460 Meals and Entertainment Customers, Suppliers		☐
6470 Utilities	Gas, Oil, Water, Electric	☐
Semi-Variable - Other		☐

A Word on Fixed and Semi-Variable Costs:

Some expenses, such as interest costs, can be either Fixed or Semi-Variable. Depending upon the industry you are in and your relationship with your suppliers, some Semi-Variable Cost types can go either way. Don't transfer the cost items from Semi-Variable categories to the Fixed section just because they happen to be Fixed at this moment. Keep the categories organized in the way you see here. For now, we are just creating organization.

The goal for the organization of your P&L is to put the right items in the right places for all the right reasons. The budget goal will be to eventually achieve an equal balance between Fixed and Semi-Variable Costs.

MONEY KEPT

The last main section of your P&L will be the Net Profit after all expenses are deducted.

There are four main purposes for your Profit: Reinvestment, Retained Earnings (savings), Corporate Taxes, and Shareholder Dividends.

We will not use account codes for Net Profit items at this time.

The biggest error that small business owners could possibly make is to think that NET PROFIT is part of their business. Technically, NET PROFIT is strictly owner money and is the RESULT of the company's effort... not a PART of the company's effort.

ACCOUNT CODE	CURRENT FINANCIAL SITUATION DESCRIPTION	MONTHLY ADJUSTED P&L	ANNUAL ADJUSTED P&L
	NET PROFIT		
REINVESTMENT EXPENSE			
RETAINED EARNINGS			
CORPORATE TAXES - Federal			
CORPORATE TAXES - State			
SHAREHOLDER DISTRIBUTION			

PUTTING THIS INTO PERSPECTIVE

What would you say if you were on vacation and expected your monthly interest payment from your stock and investment portfolio to reliably show up in your bank account as your usual direct deposit? When you go to spend the $4,000 that you normally receive, you see that only $1,200 showed up in your bank. Enraged at this, you drop your fishing pole and call furiously to customer service. The polite agent informs you that someone in the company that you own stock in decided to buy some equipment, and there isn't enough money to pay your interest this month.

As an investor, you are an owner, but not necessarily a manager in your business.

Managers are paid by business owners to make the owners a profit. When the profit is made, it is not the privilege or the responsibility of any manager to touch the owner's money. It is the responsibility of the owner, not the managers, to reinvest to keep their company safe, competitive and legally compliant.

MONEY MANAGED

It is important to understand that every little improvement you make to your P&L reduces your taxes and puts more money into your pocket. Keeping more of the money you have already made is the benefit of good accounting. So... just look at all of this as an Easter egg hunt. You aren't making corrections just to learn accounting. Everywhere you find a plastic egg, there is a sweet surprise inside.

VERIFY YOUR SUSPECTED ERRORS BEFORE TOTALLING.

On your P&L, make notations of any suspected errors that you find. You might have certain experience in an industry and are aware of specific costs that might apply to you. Always begin by making errors as suspicions. Let nothing be an error without quantifiable verification. Until you verify that there is an error and it can be measured in time or money, you shouldn't make judgements or rely on guesswork about it. Just note exactly what you see.

By using account codes, did you find anything on your P&L that requires further discussion? Further research? If so... make notes. If items are missing, write the word missing and do some research.

CREATING YOUR BALANCED BUDGET AFTER YOU HAVEADJUSTED YOUR PROFIT AND LOSS STATEMENT

So far, you have only organized your P&L. You do not have a balanced budget just yet. There are still a few more steps to take.

THE BUDGET appears slightly different than the P&L ORGANIZER. As you can see, the budget has a few more columns.

TO CREATE YOUR KANKETA BALANCED BUDGET:

1. Total all monthly ADJUSTED <u>FIXED</u> Costs that you entered on your P&L ORGANIZER.

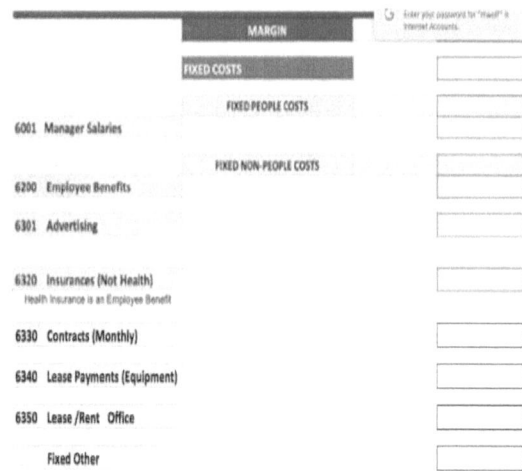

2. Total all monthly ADJUSTED <u>SEMI-VARIABLE</u> Costs that you entered on your P&L ORGANIZER.

SEMI-VARIABLE COSTS		
	SEMI-VARIABLE PEOPLE COSTS	
6001 Manager Bonuses		
	SEMI-VARIABLE NON-PEOPLE COSTS	
6400 Banking Services		
6403 Credit Card Fees		
6404 Interest		
6405 Office Supplies		
6410 Professional Services		
6420 Repairs and Maintenance (Not Vehicles)		
6430 Taxes, Business Licenses includes FUTA, SUTA, FICA matching		
6440 Vehicles - All Expenses Vehicle Operation	Gas, Oil, Maintenance, Plates, Permits	
6450 Travel, Per Diem for Business Customers, Suppliers		
6460 Meals and Entertainment Customers, Suppliers		
6470 Utilities	Gas, Oil, Water, Electric	
Semi-Variable - Other		

3. Multiply the LARGEST of these two totals by **3**. This is your new monthly BALANCED MARGIN target.

4. In your BUDGET WORKSHEET (example the next page), place your answer above in the **MARGIN** row of the column on the far right, **"100% NORMAL BUDGET"**.

DUVALL FOODS ACCOUNT CODE	LAST MONTH's PERFORMANCE BANK STATEMENTS	THIS MONTH 1st - 15th	THIS MONTH 16th - LAST	TOTAL ACTUAL MONTH TO DATE	THIS MONTH's BUDGET	100% NORMAL MONTHLY BUDGET
	MARGIN					
	FIXED COSTS					
6001 Manager Salaries	FIXED PEOPLE COSTS					
	FIXED NON PEOPLE COSTS					
6200 Employee Benefits						
6301 Advertising						
6320 Insurances (Not Health)						
Health Insurance is an Employee Benefit						
6330 Contracts (Monthly)						
6340 Lease Payments (Equipment)						
6350 Lease/Rent Office						
Fixed Other						
UNSPENT Fund						

Your MARGIN is NORMAL and balanced when...

> **1/3** of your new Margin equals your actual FIXED costs plus any UNSPENT remainder of 1/3 of the Margin

> **1/3** of your new Margin equals your actual SEMI-VARIABLE costs plus any UNSPENT remainder of 1/3 of the Margin

> **1/3** of your new Margin equals the NET PROFIT BUDGET of your business.

This is your 100% New Normal (ideal) Monthly Kanketa Balanced Budget and the best possible scenario for keeping your business safe.

Your NET SALES are NORMAL and balanced when...

5. You add your Cost of Goods Sold total (on your P&L ORGANIZER) to the new Balanced Margin Target number that you just entered to get your monthly required **NET SALES.**

Your GROSS SALES are NORMAL and balanced when...

6. You add your Cost of Quality total (best guess) on your P&L ORGANIZER to your NET SALES to get your new monthly **TARGET GROSS SALES.**

YOUR TARGET MONTHLY GROSS SALES IS YOUR "100% NORMAL BUDGET"

7. On your BUDGET Worksheet you will notice an UNSPENT box at the bottom of each of the FIXED and SEMI-VARIABLE sections. Any remaining money that was not yet budgeted in each should be entered into the UNSPENT box.

8. If you have done everything correctly, the largest of your FIXED and SEMI-VARIABLE totals should have a zero in the UNSPENT box. The lowest of your FIXED and SEMI-VARIABLE totals will have an UNSPENT amount, which is equal to the difference between your FIXED and SEMI-VARIABLE expenses.

Review:

FIXED BUDGET with UNSPENT BOX added

6320	Insurances (Not Health)				
	Health Insurance is an Employee Benefit				
6330	Contracts (Monthly)				
6340	Lease Payments (Equipment)				
6350	Lease /Rent Office				
	Fixed Other				
UNSPENT Fixed					

SEMI-VARIABLE BUDGET with UNSPENT BOX added

6450	Travel, Per Diem for Business Customers, Suppliers				
6460	Meals and Entertainment Customers, Suppliers				
6470	Utilities	Gas, Oil. Water, Electric			
	Semi-Variable - Other				
UNSPENT Semi-Variable					

CHAPTER 12

USE YOUR BALANCED BUDGET TO CREATE FINANCIAL SAFETY

ACHIEVE FINANCIAL BALANCE

Build permanent
financial safety
into your business

The Best Time to Start Is Yesterday.
The Next Best Time to Start Is Today.

Now that you have your 100% Normal budget, how do you use it?

RULE #1: FIND YOUR MONTH'S BUDGET. <u>WHAT CAN YOU REALLY AFFORD</u>?

LAST MONTH'S GROSS SALES PERFORMANCE
(Sales, not revenue)

... IS THIS MONTH's BUDGET

RULE #2: FIND THE PERFORMANCE (PERCENTAGE OF SALES) FOR THIS MONTH'S BUDGET

DIVIDE LAST MONTH'S GROSS SALES AMOUNT
BY YOUR 100% NORMAL GROSS SALES BUDGET

DUVALL FOODS / ACCOUNT CODE	LAST MONTH's PERFORMANCE BANK STATEMENTS	THIS MONTH 1st - 15th	THIS MONTH 16th - LAST	TOTAL ACTUAL MONTH TO DATE	THIS MONTH's BUDGET	100% NORMAL MONTHLY BUDGET
REVENUE DEPOSITED					$59,139	
4961 Deposits Not from Customers					$11,781	
					72%	
GROSS SALES					$47,358	$65,000
4101 CORE PRODUCTS					$16,662	$23,141
4130 BROKERED PRODUCTS					$30,138	$41,859
COST OF QUALITY					$6,028	$8,372
5100 Samples					$2,582	$3,586
5120 Returned Items					$360	$500
5140 Discounts					$2,365	$3,285
5160 Warranties					$346	$481
5180 Error and Rework					$288	$400
5190 Scrap					$86	$120
NET SALES					$37,440	$52,000

In this example, 100% NORMAL monthly budget is $65,000.

Last month's GROSS SALES performance was $47,358. (remove the pennies).

This month's budget = $47,358 divided by $65,000 = 72.8% performance

Round down by removing the tenths of a percent.

LAST MONTH'S PERFORMANCE = this month's budget
72% of NORMAL

All expenses for this month must not exceed 72% ($47,358).
Enter last month's total Gross Sales into the THIS MONTH'S BUDGET column on your Budget Worksheet.

If you are tracking your Core Products (that you produce or the staples that are routine inventory in your store), enter 72% of your 100% Normal Core Product budget. In our example, 72% of $23,141 Normal = $16,662.

If you are tracking your Brokered Products (that you occasionally buy and sell at a profit or special orders in your store), enter 72% of your 100% Normal Brokered Products budget. In our example, 72% of $41,859 Normal = $30,138.

THIS MONTH'S BUDGET FOR COST OF QUALITY
(Last Month's Performance creates this month's budget)
Example: 72% of $8,372 (100% Normal Monthly Cost of Quality budget) = $ 6,028
Enter 72% of last month's total Cost of Quality Budget into the THIS MONTH'S BUDGET column on your budget worksheet.

THIS MONTH'S BUDGET FOR NET SALES
(Last Month's Performance creates this month's budget)
Example: When you subtract your $6,028 Cost of Quality from your Gross Sales, your NET SALES will now reflect 72% of $52,000 (**100% Normal Monthly Net Sales Budget)**
= $ 37,440

THIS MONTH'S BUDGET FOR COST OF GOODS SOLD
(Last Month's Performance creates this month's budget)
Example: 72% of $20,800 (100% Normal Monthly Cost of Goods Sold budget)
= $14,976
Enter 72% of last month's total Cost of Goods Sold Budget into the THIS MONTH'S BUDGET column on your budget worksheet.

ACCOUNT CODE	LAST MONTH's PERFORMANCE BANK STATEMENTS	MONTHLY 1st - 15th	MONTHLY 16th - LAST	TOTAL MONTH TO DATE	LAST MONTH's PERFORMANCE	100% NORMAL BUDGET
COST OF GOODS SOLD					$14,976	$20,800
5201 DIRECT LABOR (individuals)					$7,600	$10,555
5301 Supplies (disposable)					$1,279	$1,777
5303 Materials for Resale					$2,160	$3,000
5320 Raw Materials (mfg)					$0	$0
5340 Packaging (supplies & services)					$1,734	$2,408
5360 Merchandise (for Resale)					$0	$0
5367 Services (for Resale)					$785	$1,090

Code	Description					Amount 1	Amount 2
5400	Commissions					$0	$0
5440	Direct Labor Benefits					$0	$0
5650	Rentals					$320	$444
5600	Contracted Services (Companies)					$0	$0
5700	Delivery & Shipping					$654	$908
5750	Sales Tax					$0	
5752	Equip Parts (mfg) Equip Resale					$0	
5753	Uniforms, Wearables					$445	$618
5799	Cost of Goods - OTHER					$0	

THIS MONTH'S BUDGET FOR MARGIN
(Last Month's Performance creates this month's budget)
Example: 72% of $31,200 (100% Normal Monthly MARGIN budget)
= $22,464
Enter 72% of last month's MARGIN into THIS MONTH'S BUDGET column on your budget worksheet.

ACCOUNT CODE	LAST MONTH's PERFORMANCE BANK STATEMENTS	MONTHLY 1st - 15th	MONTHLY 16th - LAST	TOTAL MONTH TO DATE	LAST MONTH's PERFORMANCE	100% NORMAL BUDGET
	MARGIN				$22,464	$31,200
	FIXED COSTS				$10,400	$10,400
6001 Manager Salaries	FIXED PEOPLE COSTS	Paid by the 10th			$5,204	$5,200
	FIXED NON-PEOPLE COSTS				$5,200	$5,200
6200 Employee Benefits					$1,000	$1,000
6301 Advertising					$1,298	$1,298
6320 Insurances (Not Health) Health Insurance is an Employee Benefit					$875	$875
6330 Contracts (Monthly)					$572	$572
6340 Lease Payments (Equipment)					$405	$405
6350 Lease /Rent Office					$750	$750
Fixed Other						

THIS MONTH'S BUDGET FOR FIXED COSTS REMAINS THE SAME AS 100% NORMAL (Last Month's Performance)
Unspent: You do not have to always spend the entire balanced budget. Spend what you need to up to the budget amount.

FIXED PEOPLE COSTS (managers)
Example:
Pay your Managers $5,200 (½ of their Normal salaries) by the 15th as always. No change from month to month.

FIXED NON-PEOPLE COSTS (monthly operating overhead)
Example:
Pay all Fixed Non-People operating expenses up to your Normal Fixed Non-People budget by the 15th. No change from month to month.

THIS MONTH'S BUDGET FOR SEMI-VARIABLE PEOPLE COSTS
(Last Month's Performance creates this month's budget)
Example: 72% of $10,400 (100% Normal Monthly MARGIN budget)
= $7,488
Enter 72% of last month's MARGIN into THIS MONTH'S BUDGET column on your budget worksheet.

I understand that until now you have always paid your managers a fixed monthly salary. The problem: This is a new day and a new normal. If you are to rebuild your company, get it safe and keep it safe, that old habit is now worn and dated.

YOU MUST insist that one half of all manager pay will be Fixed salaries that do not change (payroll period #1 of the month) and one half of all manager pay will be Semi-Variable pay for performance of the company (payroll period #2 of the month). If you do not do this, you will run into cashflow problems.

Call a meeting. Be humbly transparent. Stay in control. Be courageous. Offer the deal. Get agreement. Collaborate on how to get your company back to normal. Keep the managers that will help you.

Don't allow your Direct Labor workers to think that they are on a Fixed salary. They aren't. Don't hire managers who won't cooperate.

Hard choices today. A safe business for tomorrow.

ACCOUNT CODE	LAST MONTH's PERFORMANCE BANK STATEMENTS	MONTHLY 1st - 15th	MONTHLY 16th - LAST	TOTAL MONTH TO DATE	LAST MONTH's PERFORMANCE	100% NORMAL BUDGET
	SEMI-VARIABLE COSTS				$7,488	$10,400
6001 Manager (Performance Pay) On	SEMI-VARIABLE PEOPLE COSTS	Paid by the 25th			$3,744	$5,200
	SEMI-VARIABLE NON-PEOPLE COSTS				$3,744	$5,200
6400 Banking Services					$174	$241
6403 Credit Card Fees					$73	$102
6404 Interest					$474	$658
6405 Office Supplies					$423	$588
6410 Professional Services					$468	$650
6420 Repairs and Maintenance (Not Vehicles)					$55	$77
6430 Taxes, Business Licenses includes FUTA, SUTA, FICA matching					$1,322	$1,836
6440 Vehicles - All Expenses Vehicle Operation	Gas, Oil, Maintenance, Plates, Permits				$449	$623
6450 Travel, Per Diem for Business Customers, Suppliers					$233	$324
6460 Meals and Entertainment Customers, Suppliers					$12	$17
6470 Utilities	Gas, Oil, Water, Electric				$349	$485
Semi-Variable - Other						
UNSPENT Semi-Variable						

THIS MONTH'S BUDGET FOR SEMI-VARIABLE NON-PEOPLE COSTS
(Last Month's Performance creates this month's budget)
Example: 72% of $10,400 (100% Normal Monthly MARGIN budget) = $7,488

Enter 72% of last month's MARGIN into THIS MONTH'S BUDGET column on your budget worksheet.

FIND YOUR MONTH-END NET PROFIT

FROM LAST MONTH's MARGIN...

Subtract your total Fixed Costs for last month.

Subtract your total Semi-Variable Costs for last month.

The answer is your true Net Profit for last month (same process applies to any monthly sales performance level).

Example:

Last Month's Margin performance (72% Margin of $31,200 Margin at Normal = $22,4640)

minus the Fixed Costs of $10,400 that do not change,

minus the Semi-Variable Costs (72% of $10,400 that do change) = $7,488

Enter 72% of last month's MARGIN into THIS MONTH'S BUDGET column on your budget worksheet.

Example: YOUR NET PROFIT BUDGET should begin the month looking like this

DUVALL FOODS ACCOUNT CODE	LAST MONTH's PERFORMANCE BANK STATEMENTS	THIS MONTH 1st - 15th	THIS MONTH 16th - LAST	TOTAL ACTUAL MONTH TO DATE	THIS MONTH's BUDGET	100% NORMAL MONTHLY BUDGET
NET PROFIT					$7,488	$10,400
25% REINVESTMENT EXPENSE					$1,872	$2,600
25% RETAINED EARNINGS					$1,872	$650
CORPORATE TAXES - Federal 17%					$1,273	$1,768
CORPORATE TAXES - State 8%					$599	$832
25% SHAREHOLDER DISTRIBUTION					$1,872	$2,600

Example: YOUR BUDGET should begin the month looking like this

DUVALL FOODS ACCOUNT CODE	LAST MONTH's PERFORMANCE BANK STATEMENTS	THIS MONTH 1st - 15th	THIS MONTH 16th - LAST	TOTAL ACTUAL MONTH TO DATE	THIS MONTH's BUDGET	100% NORMAL MONTHLY BUDGET
REVENUE DEPOSITED					$59,139	
4961 Deposits Not from Customers					$11,781	
					72%	
	GROSS SALES				$47,358	$65,000
4101 CORE PRODUCTS					$16,862	$23,141
4130 BROKERED PRODUCTS					$30,138	$41,859
	COST OF QUALITY				$6,028	$8,372
5100 Samples					$2,582	$3,586
5120 Returned Items					$360	$500
5140 Discounts					$2,365	$3,285
5160 Warranties					$346	$481
5180 Error and Rework					$288	$400
5190 Scrap					$86	$120
	NET SALES				$37,440	$52,000
	COST OF GOODS SOLD				$14,976	$20,800
5201 DIRECT LABOR (individuals)					$7,600	$10,556
5301 Supplies (disposable)					$1,279	$1,777
5303 Materials for Resale					$2,160	$3,000
5320 Raw Materials (mfg)					$0	$0
5340 Packaging (supplies & services)					$1,734	$2,408
5360 Merchandise (for Resale)					$0	$0
5367 Services (for Resale)					$785	$1,090
5400 Commissions					$0	$0
5440 Direct Labor Benefits					$0	$0
5650 Rentals					$320	$444
5600 Contracted Services (Companies)					$0	$0
5700 Delivery & Shipping					$654	$908
5750 Sales Tax					$0	
5752 Equip Parts (mfg) Equip Resale					$0	
5753 Uniforms, Wearables					$445	$618
5799 Cost of Goods - OTHER					$0	

ACCOUNT CODE	LAST MONTH's PERFORMANCE BANK STATEMENTS	MONTHLY 1st - 15th	MONTHLY 16th - LAST	TOTAL MONTH TO DATE	LAST MONTH's PERFORMANCE	100% NORMAL BUDGET
	MARGIN				$22,464	$31,200
	FIXED COSTS				$10,400	$10,400
6001 Manager Salaries	FIXED PEOPLE COSTS	Paid by the 10th			$5,204	$5,200
	FIXED NON-PEOPLE COSTS				$5,200	$5,200
6200 Employee Benefits					$1,000	$1,000
6301 Advertising					$1,298	$1,298
6320 Insurances (Not Health) — Health Insurance is an Employee Benefit					$875	$875
6330 Contracts (Monthly)					$572	$572
6340 Lease Payments (Equipment)					$405	$405
6350 Lease /Rent Office					$750	$750
6351 Fixed Costs Other						
UNSPENT Fixed					$300	$300

ACCOUNT CODE	LAST MONTH's PERFORMANCE BANK STATEMENTS	MONTHLY 1st - 15th	MONTHLY 16th - LAST	TOTAL MONTH TO DATE	LAST MONTH's PERFORMANCE	100% NORMAL BUDGET
	SEMI-VARIABLE COSTS				$7,119	$10,400
6001 Manager Bonuses	SEMI-VARIABLE PEOPLE COSTS					$5,200
	SEMI-VARIABLE NON-PEOPLE COSTS					$5,200
6430 Banking Services					$226	$241
6433 Credit Card Fees					$99	$112
6434 Interest					$837	$938
6435 Office Supplies					$668	$668
6410 Professional Services					$950	$950
6420 Repairs and Maintenance (Not Vehicle)					$120	$77
6430 Taxes, Business Licenses — includes FUTA, SUTA, FICA matching					$1,256	$1,036
6440 Vehicles - All Expenses — Vehicle Operation	Gas, Oil, Maintenance, Plates, Permits				$513	$603
6450 Travel, Per Diem for Business — Customers, Suppliers					$121	$324
6460 Meals and Entertainment — Customers, Suppliers					$93	$17
6470 Utilities	Gas, Oil, Water, Electric				$465	$465
Semi-Variable - Other						
UNSPENT Semi-Variable						

DUVALL FOODS	LAST MONTH's PERFORMANCE	MONTHLY	MONTHLY	TOTAL	LAST MONTH's	100% NORMAL
ACCOUNT CODE	BANK STATEMENTS	1st - 15th	16th - LAST	MONTH TO DATE	PERFORMANCE	MONTHLY BUDGET
NET PROFIT					- $7,118	$10,400
25% REINVESTMENT EXPENSE					$1,780	$2,600
25% RETAINED EARNINGS					$445	$650
CORPORATE TAXES - Federal 17%					$1,210	$1,768
CORPORATE TAXES - State 8%					$569	$832
25% SHAREHOLDER DISTRIBUTION					$3,114	$2,600

Bank and Card Statements are More Truthful Than QuickBooks.

Certainly, you may use accounting software such as QuickBooks, Xero, etc., for record-keeping purposes. However, your most accurate tool for tracking actual expenses is your banking activity that appears on your bank statements. Only your bank can legitimately verify exactly what you have already spent without any error.

Two Birds. One Stone.

Small businesses rely too heavily on their accountants to categorize and classify their income and expenses. Your accountant must do guesswork to make sense of things. The guesses can be wrong and cost you a lot of money. Failure to provide your accountant with timely, accurate, legible, and complete information can get expensive and lead to unnecessary errors and significant tax expenses. This actual expense-to-budget comparison eliminates this problem. By marking up your bank statements every two weeks, you still remember what each expense was. "Hmm, we went to Qdoba and met with Cindy that Tuesday for a project review lunch." Waiting until the end of the year is downright impossible, probably inaccurate, or at the very least, a lot more stress and headache than spending 10 minutes every two weeks to make a few notes.

The best news of all: You are operating your business safely for the most possible profit now, and resale (or lease) value later.

The balanced budget items are simply a list of the main income and expense tax categories that the IRS looks at on your tax return. Kanketa has reorganized the IRS expense categories and separated them into tax codes for Cost of Quality, Cost of Goods Sold, Fixed, and Semi-Variable expenses.

Using your bank statements to do an actual-to-budget comparison twice a month. At the end of the year, you will have **12** monthly budget comparisons on file with every expense properly and accurately identified. There is no guesswork by your accountant, and you are all set for any IRS audit.

PRINT YOUR BUSINESS CHECKBOOK BANK ACTIVITY TWICE A MONTH:

On the 16th of the month, or just after, print your bank activity for the period from the 1st through the 15th.

Using your Account Codes, identify each type of expense on your bank statement.

Repeat this process just after the 1st day of the following month, with bank activity for the period from the 16th to the last day of the previous month.

Using your Account Codes, identify each type of expense <u>on your bank statement.</u>

MARK UP YOUR BANK STATEMENTS.

Identify all of your Income and expenses for the period. Your statement will look something like this:

Date	Description	Code / Note	Amount
03/29/2019	Andys On Good Homilwaukee Wi	6460 meals	$37.73
03/28/2019	Web Authorized Pmt Cardmember Serv	6301 web design	$239.95
03/28/2019	Debit Purchase -visa 03/27 card Abra - 5513 Milwmilwaukee Wi	6405 Office	$450.00
03/28/2019	Debit Purchase -visa 03/27 card 668 Elevator Equipme323-2450147 Ca	6420 Repair	$151.55
03/28/2019	Debit Purchase -visa 03/27 card 6(Speedway 04289 Mmilwaukee Wi	6440 Gas	$37.81
03/28/2019	Misc Credit Merch 8032524855 Milwauke [	6301 Advertising $250.00	
03/27/2019	Debit Purchase -visa 03/26 card 6(Walgreens #12524brown Deer Wi	6405 Office Supplies	$71.39
03/27/2019	Electronic Deposit Dak Properties l	6330 contract $518.75	
03/26/2019	Electronic Withdrawal Irs	6430 taxes	$2,626.04
03/25/2019	Check View Image	4130 brokered 1220	$1,000.00
03/25/2019	Electronic Withdrawal Timewarnerwis	6330 contract	$89.75
03/25/2019	Debit Purchase - Visa 03/24 card 7! Jobber Httpsgetjobbca	6330 contract	$67.00
03/25/2019	Debit Purchase -visa 03/21 card 66 Access Electroni301-645-1733md	5700 Shipping	$261.07
03/25/2019	Debit Purchase -visa 03/21 card Frontera Grill Bchicago Il	6460 Client Entertainment	$24.53
03/25/2019	Deposit View Image	4101 CORE Products $2,483.75	

GROUP AND TOTAL YOUR LIKE-ITEMS.

Example: In the above bank statement you would add the 6405 office items together. You would add the 6330 contract items together, etc.

ENTER ALL BANK STATEMENT ITEM AMOUNTS, AND LIKE-ITEM TOTALS into their respective rows in the budget for the current period:

For the 1st through the 15th

For the 16th through the last day of the month

EXAMPLE: BALANCED BUDGET BEING USED MONTHLY WITH BANK STATEMENTS

DUVALL FOODS ACCOUNT CODE	LAST MONTH's PERFORMANCE BANK STATEMENTS	THIS MONTH 1st - 15th	THIS MONTH 16th - LAST	TOTAL ACTUAL MONTH TO DATE	THIS MONTH's BUDGET	100% NORMAL MONTHLY BUDGET
REVENUE DEPOSITED					$59,139	
4961 Deposits Not from Customers					$11,781	
				(68% actual)	72%	
	GROSS SALES	$17,390	$14,814	$32,203	$47,358	$65,000
4101 CORE PRODUCTS		$6,118	$5,212	$11,330	$16,662	$23,141
4130 BROKERED PRODUCTS		$11,067	$9,427	$20,444	$30,138	$41,859
	COST OF QUALITY	$2,213	$1,885	$4,099	$6,028	$8,372
5100 Samples		$948	$808	$1,756	$2,582	$3,586
5120 Returned Items		$132	$113	$245	$360	$500
5140 Discounts		$868	$740	$1,608	$2,365	$3,285
5160 Warranties		$127	$108	$235	$346	$481
5180 Error and Rework		$106	$90	$196	$288	$400
5190 Scrap		$52	$27	$69	$86	$120
	NET SALES	$13,748	$11,711	$25,459	$37,440	$52,000

DUVALL FOODS ACCOUNT CODE	LAST MONTH's PERFORMANCE BANK STATEMENTS	THIS MONTH 1st - 15th	THIS MONTH 16th - LAST	TOTAL ACTUAL MONTH TO DATE	THIS MONTH's BUDGET	100% NORMAL MONTHLY BUDGET
COST OF GOODS SOLD		$6,499	$4,684	$10,184	$14,976	$20,800
5201 DIRECT LABOR (individuals)		$3,321	$2,829	$6,251	$9,045	$10,555
5301 Supplies (disposable)		$447	$381	$828	$1,218	$1,777
5303 Materials for Resale		$756	$644	$1,349	$2,058	$3,000
5320 Raw Materials (mfg)		$0	$0		$0	$0
5340 Packaging (supplies & services)		$371	$316	$687	$1,010	$2,408
5360 Merchandise (for Resale)		$112	$95	$207	$305	$0
5367 Services (for Resale)		$621	$444	$1,065	$1,419	$1,090
5400 Commissions		$184	$156	$340	$500	$0
5440 Direct Labor Benefits		$0	$0	$0	$0	$0
5650 Rentals		$40	$35	$75	$110	$444
5600 Contracted Services (Companies)		$388	$330	$718	$1,066	$0
5700 Delivery & Shipping		$200	$170	$370	$544	$908
5750 Sales Tax		$0	$0	$0		
5752 Equip Parts (mfg) Equip Resale		$0	$0	$0		
5753 Uniforms, Wearables		$225	$192	$418	$614	$618
5799 Cost of Goods - OTHER		$41	$35	$76	$112	

ACCOUNT CODE	LAST MONTH's PERFORMANCE BANK STATEMENTS	MONTHLY 1st - 15th	MONTHLY 16th - LAST	TOTAL MONTH TO DATE	LAST MONTH's PERFORMANCE	100% NORMAL BUDGET
	MARGIN	$0,080	$7,715	$7,180	$21,054	$31,200
	FIXED COSTS	$4,745			$9,885	$10,400
6001 Manager Salaries	FIXED PEOPLE COSTS	$5,300		$5,300	$5,304	$5,300
	FIXED NON-PEOPLE COSTS	$4,064		$4,064	$4,952	$5,200
6200 Employee Benefits		$683		$685	$982	$1,000
6301 Advertising		$000		$000	$1,120	$1,200
6330 Insurances (Not Health)	$69	$893	$14	$911	$800
Health Insurance is an Employee Benefit						
6330 Contracts (Monthly)		$472		$472	$472	$472
6340 Lease Payments (Equipment)		$60	$405	$465	$465	$465
6350 Lease /Rent Office		$725		$725	$750	$725
Fixed Other		$0	$22	$22	$212	$0
UNSPENT Fixed					$300	$300
	SEMI-VARIABLE COSTS	$608	$5,351	$5,960	$9,885	$10,400
6001 Manager Bonuses	SEMI-VARIABLE PEOPLE COSTS		$4,706	$4,706	$3,766	$5,200
	SEMI-VARIABLE NON-PEOPLE COSTS		$1,0	$1,0	$3,766	$5,200
6400 Banking Services		$10	$0	$10	$226	$241
6400 Credit Card Fees			$05	$05	$58	$102
6404 Interest		$99	$67	$675	$837	$950
6405 Office Supplies			$05	$05	$866	$598
6410 Professional Services			$650	$650	$850	$850
6420 Repairs and Maintenance (Not Vehicles)		$11	$0	$11	$120	$77
6430 Taxes, Business Licenses includes FUTA, SUTA, FICA matching			$77	$77	$1,745	$1,836
6440 Vehicles - All Expenses Vehicle Operation	Gas, Oil, Maintenance, Plates, Permits		$05	$05	$513	$423
6450 Travel, Per Diem for Business Customers, Suppliers			$0	$0	$127	$324
6460 Meals and Entertainment Customers, Suppliers		$44	$0	$44	$23	$17
6470 Utilities	Gas, Oil, Water, Electric	$05	$0	$05	$666	$695
Semi-Variable - Other			$0	$0	$0	$0
UNSPENT Semi-Variable						$300

Mike Wolf

	NET PROFIT	$9,960	$9,885	$10,400
25% REINVESTMENT EXPENSE		$2,490	$2,471	$2,600
25% RETAINED EARNINGS		$622	$618	$650
CORPORATE TAXES - Federal 17%		$956	$1,680	$1,768
CORPORATE TAXES - State 8%		$0	$791	$832
25% SHAREHOLDER DISTRIBUTION		$2,490	$4,325	$2,600

OVER BUDGET

What expenses are you over budget?

Why?

Is this a trend?

You must only budget one time every year. <u>DO NOT</u> re-budget in the middle of a year under any circumstance. It will give you a false reading for the following year.

What can be done?
(If so, you might have to increase your budget for that item by using some of your UNSPENT budget if you have it available.
What Fixed expenses can you convert to Semi-Variable?
What Semi-Variable expenses can you convert to Fixed?

What can you **negotiate?**
What can you **combine?**
What can you **eliminate?**
What can you **outsource?**
What can you **rethink?**
What can you **reassign?**

With month-to-month budget management, you will have just done most of your accountant's work and your year-end tax preparation bill should be very small.

Every adjustment and correction that you have made to your P&L adds no less than 17% of the face amount of the correction to your personal income earnings for the year. Higher amounts up to 30% are possible depending upon the amount of your Margin.

WHAT IS YOUR TIME WORTH?

This brings me to a bigger question. What about you? My answer is: It depends upon who you are at the moment.

If you are a production worker in your own company
You are out in the shop or you are working in a Workroom IN your business, you are worth what you can hire someone else to do. Keep in mind that while you are worth the average industry hourly labor rate to your company as a contracted worker your hourly value is actually worth your last year's tax amount filed personally divided by 1,000.

If you are a Workroom Manager in your own company
As a Workroom Manager hired by the Business Leader of the company (who might be you) to manage two Workroom corridors, your Fixed wage per month is 4.17% of Margin at 100% Normal to maintain the Workroom performance, and 4.17% of Margin multiplied by the previous month's performance column percent of Normal to grow your Workroom.

If you are the Business Leader of your company
You might be the Business Leader who is managing your company, hired by the owner (who might be you) to manage the owner's company (which might be yours).

As a Business Leader, your time is worth the man minute cost of one-third of the Margin of a management company of the owner that you might work for.

Half of the Business Leader's Fixed salary is paid for maintaining the performance of the operating company (which right now is your company). The other half of the Business Leader's Performance Compensation is for your ability to grow your company through good leadership.

The Business Leader's man minute cost is the Net Profit of your company at Normal divided by 8,400 minutes a month.

If you are the owner of your company...

then, forget all of this and divide your last year's taxable income by 1,000 to get your hourly value as the owner of your business. Up to 1,000 hours a year is the amount of time that you as the owner has available to work ON your business, creating strategies, processes and procedures for your Business Leader to carry out.

Example: If you filed taxes on $85,000 last year, your time this year is worth $85 an hour.

If you are a company of one, you are the owner, and the management team of your company. Every activity, every task no matter how small is costing your business your personal hourly value.

"How much stock (or shares) should I give to investors?"

Don't add non-participating investors who do not contribute skills and guidance, is the best answer I can give. Accept no passive investors with excuses and stories for why they can't put in more than money. Look closely at what Net Profit you are permanently giving away to a passive investor. You might not have enough profit left to satisfy either of you.

Only if you must:

DEFINE: 10% to the individual who dreamed up the concept of the business

IDENTIFY: 10% to the individual who identified the markets and all resources needed

LOCATE: 10% to the individual who specifically located the markets and the resources needed

QUALIFY: 10% to the individual who contacted the individual resources to understand how the relationship would work (time, team, money)

PROPOSE: 10% to the individual who formalized the key supplier agreements in writing

CLOSE: 10% to the individual who attracts enough potential prospects to launch the business once it's set up

DESIGN: 10% to the individual who designed all work responsibilities for employees and vendors

DEVELOP: 10% to the individual who developed the (written) systems to operate the company

IMPLEMENT: 10% to the individual (Business Leader) who is responsible to carry out the plan and put the systems into profitable action

MANAGE: 10% to the individual who continues to ensure and report progress to the owner of the company

---

= 100% SHAREHOLDER EQUITY

In Kanketa there are no passive money-only investor-shareholders in companies of fewer than 30 employees. Keep your shares. Use your profit to repay a Start-Up loan and avoid passive investors. There are a million less expensive ways to get money besides permanently paying your hard-earned profit to non-participating investors.

"What is my breakeven point?"

When your monthly **MARGIN** is at exactly 50% of your Normal (not 51%), you are at breakeven. Even then, your bills are covered for three months, until you figure out how to rescue yourself. Breakeven is the only place where you make absolutely zero dollars of Net Profit.

If you have one dollar or more above exactly 50%, you have made a profit, no matter how small. When your sales fall into the "Zone of Recovery", you are highly dependent upon your ability to balance your finances. This is where Balanced Budgeting becomes critical.

Also, growth – too much or too fast – can push you into the "Zone of Indifference".
This is another danger point since, mathematically you are being drained of cash.
(Hello, Toys-R-Us, Kmart and Sears!)

> **Kanketa breakeven is exactly 50% of Net Sales. In Kanketa, the business is sustainable for three consecutive months during a business interruption.**

True Story: Growing too fast is not growing at all

Michael's manufacturing company in Minot, North Dakota produced quality sawblades. He had more orders than is 11-person shop could handle. One day, a global company offered to double his business within six months.

Michael jumped at the chance. His company was already three weeks out in deliveries. He accepted even more orders and his team found themselves working twelve-hour days.

Michael was making a good profit, but every dime of his profit was being reinvested in Cost of Goods for the new orders. His receivables were further and further out.

Michael was not able to borrow enough to keep up. His delivery times were becoming unreasonably long and the global company was growing increasingly impatient. Finally, production was so late, that the global customer was forced to buy his company just to fulfill its own production commitment.

After 17 years in his own business, Michael ended up with a job at the global company where he works today.

Annual sales growth and consequently Margin increase beyond 20% per year is mathematically not sustainable. Net Profit must always exceed the cost of annual sales growth by no less than one third of annual Margin at 100% Normal.

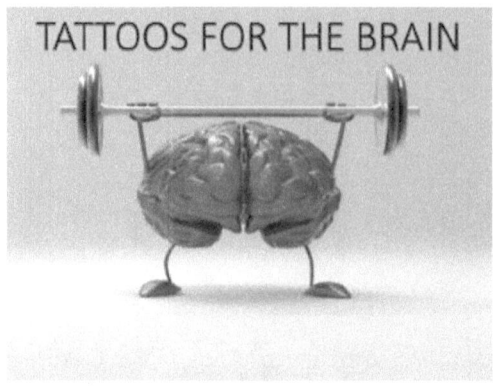

TATTOOS FOR THE BRAIN

THREE NET PROFIT TATTOOS FOR THE BALANCED BUDGET BRAIN

Here are three main takeaways for the use of your Kanketa Balanced Budget.

#1. Organize all income and expenses on your P&L in the Kanketa Balanced Budget format.

#2. At the end of every month, use your P&L to compare your total actual month's expenses with your last month's expense budget.

#3. Subtract your actual month end expenses from your total previous month's sales to get your previous month's Net Profit.

This is the very best thing you can do with your Profit and Loss Statement.

IN A WORD

During my professional career I have owned 26 businesses of every size, shape and dimension: manufacturing, business-to-business services, distribution, wholesale, retail, nonprofit, onshore, offshore, in the air, a company of three, and a company of 103. I started companies from scratch, bought them, managed them, sold them, merged and unmerged them, leased them out, partnered in them – you name it.

In most cases, I have applied every instruction in this book. Early in the game I wasn't as skillful with these practices and had limited success. Through decades of constant refinement, I became more confident as I saw my Kanketa management skills improve. By the 1990s, the results were consistent, reliable and the outcomes were astounding.

The Biggest Problem with a Small Business

It's small. Many small business owners believe that they are their business. They think that if they go way, their business goes away. "I might as well do it myself. It just won't be done right unless I've got my hands in it. You just can't get good help these days," is a common refrain.

They must touch every product, write every check, and guide every move. They mistrust everything and everyone. Their accountant can't do it right. Suppliers are lurking in every corner, always ready to take them for a ride. Their customers are constantly beating them down on price. Their undeserving competitors are getting all the jobs. All along, their handful of incompetent employees are robbing them blind.

And on, and on, and on.

Most of this is simply not true. In hundreds of candid conversations with business owners big and small I've found well-intended, quality-minded, honest, hard-working individuals who are willing to do what it takes to help their customers, vendors and employees grow and become better off. Many are searching for the answers that you have found in this book. The common thread is good intentions.

To those who believe that they <u>are</u> their business, let me say that the reality is that the government sees every business as a FEIN number (Federal Employee Identification Number). Every business is a living, breathing entity that is subject to the same operating rules, same tax laws, banking regulations, and the same compliance requirements. Al's Bait Shop, in every way, must observe the same rules as Amazon, Google and General Motors. The only difference between them is the priorities of the owner and how the businesses are managed.

A small company of ten people has the same functional demands as a single department in a medium-size company of a hundred. A medium-size company of a hundred operates functionally like a single department in a large company of thousands. The small company sells to an outside customer. The small department in a large company sells its services to an inside customer. The small business manages a checkbook. The small department in a large company treats a budget like a checkbook. The small business owner makes a profit. The small department in a large company is a profit center that shares in the profit. It's all the same stuff in a different wrapper.

As I mentioned earlier, there are millions of companies that are doing just fine without Kanketa Financial Balance. You're feeding your family. You're putting the kids through school. You get away now and then. If you have no money problems or frustrations, then again, please, you should toss this book into a shredder. This is about reducing money worries and making your life easier.

Achieving Financial Balance is an action plan that you can put into motion immediately to get on track with where you want to be with your money matters.

I hope that you explore this information further and experiment with it in your own business. It might change your life.

It changed mine.

Questions? Need help with any of this? Call 888-679-4410, ext. 1.

www.ingramcontent.com/pod-product-compliance
Lightning Source LLC
Chambersburg PA
CBHW021402210526
45463CB00001B/193